STEPHEN ELLIOTT WELCH
OF THE
HAMPTON LEGION

edited by

John Michael Priest

 BURD STREET PRESS

This Burd Street Press publication
was printed by
Beidel Printing House, Inc.
63 West Burd Street
Shippensburg, PA 17257 USA

The acid-free paper used in this book meets the guidelines for permanence and durability of the Committee on Production Guidelines for Book Longevity of the Council on Library Resources.

For a complete list of available publications
please write
Burd Street Press
Division of White Mane Publishing Company, Inc.
P. O. Box 152
Shippensburg, PA 17257 USA

Library of Congress Cataloging-in-Publication Data

Stephen Elliott Welch of the Hampton Legion / edited by John Michael Priest.
    p.   cm. -- (Civil War heritage series ; v. 3)
    Includes bibliographical references and index.
    ISBN 0-942597-66-4 : $12.00
    1. Welch, Stephen Elliott, b. 1843.   2. Confederate States of America. Army. Hampton Legion--Biography. 3. Soldiers--South Carolina--Biography. 4. United States--History--Civil War, 1861-1865--Campaigns. I. Priest, John M., 1949-   . II. Series.
E547.H2W377   1994
973.7'457'092--dc20   94-10652
                                         CIP

TABLE OF CONTENTS

Acknowledgements

This wonderful set of letters would not be available to the public were it not for the cooperation of the staff of the Special Collections Department, of the William R. Perkins Library, Duke University. My thanks to them for allowing me to edit these papers for publication.

Once again the staff at Antietam National Battlefield assisted me greatly by letting me search through the files of their library.

The Charleston Library Society and the Charleston County Library provided me with family history and newspaper articles about Elliott Welch and his brother, Harry.

Special thanks go to my family who lost so much of my time when I began preparing these letters for publication.

To the memory of my father,
Ira Lee Priest,
(formerly Pfc., Headquarters Company, 2nd Battalion, 1st Marines, 1st Marine Division), who taught me never to forget the individual soldier's contribution to history.

Chapter One

FROM CHARLESTON (1861)
THROUGH THE TENNESSEE CAMPAIGN (1863)

Stephen Elliott Welch, whom his family affectionately called Ellie, was born in Philadelphia, Pennsylvania on January 12, 1843, to Samuel B. and Eliza W. (Laing) Welch.[1] Charleston born and bred Samuel, a bookbinder by trade, who was visiting the city at that time, decided to take up residence there. In 1845 Eliza gave birth to their third child, William (Willie) Hawkins Welch. (An older daughter, Annie, was not living at home during the 1860 census but rejoined the family during the war.) Two years later Samuel (Sammie) B. Welch was born into an ever enlarging family.

The Welch family returned to their native Charleston, South Carolina in 1848. In 1849, Caroline W. Welch was born, followed two years later by Henry (Harry) F. Welch, who was born on August 13, 1851. The family did not have any more children until 1859 at which time Eliza bore Robbie L. Welch.

By 1860, Samuel B. Welch had become a prosperous businessman, who employed his eldest son, Elliott, in the family business. Sometime between 1860 and 1862 the family celebrated the birth of still another child —Theodore. (Theodore apparently died as an infant or a toddler because Elliott Welch never mentioned him in any letters after February 1863.) Samuel B. Welch provided his family with a quality education and Eliza insisted on good penmanship, correct spelling, and proper form, indicative of a family aware of its social status and of the value of a sound education.

In January 1861, shortly before his eighteenth birthday, Stephen Elliott Welch and William Hawkins Welch (age 16) enlisted

---

1 "S. C. Birthday," *Charleston News and Courier*, January 12, 1949, 12.

in the elite Charleston Zouave cadets. Willie was elected company 1st sergeant while Elliott became the 2nd sergeant. Both were present on Morris Island in Charleston Harbor on January 9, 1861, when the Confederate battery, which was located there, drove the Federal supply ship, *Star of the West*, away from Fort Sumter. April 12-13, 1861 found both brothers on Sullivan Island (Charleston Harbor) to observe the bombardment and the capitulation of the fort into Confederate hands.

After July 21, 1861, the brothers parted company. Willie stayed with the Charleston Zouaves which had drawn the duty of guarding Federal prisoners from Manassas. On August 7, 1861 Elliott enlisted in the South Carolina Zouaves, a company which was being formed to augment the badly battered Hampton Legion of Manassas fame. One month later, Elliott took the oath to join the Confederate States' service for the duration of the war and promptly became 1st sergeant of Company H, Hampton Legion.

Shortly thereafter, the company moved inland and northwest to Columbia, South Carolina where a measles epidemic kept it quarantined for several months. Miraculously, the company lost no lives to the feared disease.

May 1862 found the company along the Stono River below Charleston from where the strong willed Elliott Welch wrote his first surviving wartime letter.

> *Church Flats, [Stono River near Charleston, S.C.]*[2]
>
> *Sunday, May 18th 1862*

My dear Sister,[3]

Your kind note of the 12th came to hand the other day. I was happy to hear from you. We are still in the Guard House and perhaps will remain for sometime; this afternoon we expect to hear our sentences; some probably will be liberated but others will

---

2   Church Flats is located on the Stono River several miles southwest of Charleston.
Clement A. Evans, (ed.), *Confederate Military History Extended Edition*, "South Carolina," VI, (Wilmington: Broadfoot Publishing, 1987), map, between 296-297.

3   This letter is to Welch's oldest sister, Annie, who was not living at home during the 1860 census.

be punished, we hear some rumors that [Private] Geo. [Gelling] & I are to be severely handled but we are not afraid — our hearts are bold and we do not care what man can do.[4]

We had a very heavy thunderstorm today accompanied by a considerable amount of rain. It is by no means pleasant to be left so lonely as to have but 4 or 5 classmates. I am glad Mother is not going away from the city [Charleston, South Carolina]; it is useless to go away from a danger that is in the distance.

The loss of the Steamer Planter is a very great one indeed to the State, particularly, as it was lost through negligence; such offenses should be severely punished.[5]

Our Capt. [L. Cheves McCord] went down to town yesterday to get our money but this morning someone told us he had not got it & such I believe to be the case.[6] *He is not over anxious to have us paid off.*

This afternoon some of our men are engaged in removing some cannon, so you see Sunday is not strictly observed in camp. Today our noble commander saw one of the sentinels open our door to let a man bring our dinner to us & hold the door open for several minutes when he flew into a passion and ordered the poor fellow to be put on four hours extra duty (which is very severe punishment) he also told the sentinel he had a mind to put him in the Guard House. This is continually the case but we hope to have satisfaction after the War, if our lifes are spared.

---

4   A survey of the company roster shows 1st Sergeant Stephen Elliott Welch, 2nd Sergeant Donald J. Auld, and 3rd Sergeant George B. Gelling being reduced to the ranks in the summer of 1862 for charges which are not stated. Privates H. F. Fleishman and W. D. Fogle were court martialed on April 29, 1862 for charges which did not get stated in the surviving records.

Harold B. Simpson, *Hood's Texas Brigade: A Compendium*, (Hillsboro, TX: Hill Junior College, 1977), 448, 449.

5   On May 13, 1862, just before daylight, while the white captain, mate, and engineer were AWOL in Charleston, five of the eight black crew men shanghaied the vessel. Robert Small, leader of the mutineers, sailed the ship out of Charleston Harbor and delivered it to the U.S. Navy's blockade squadron. The Confederacy lost a 24 pounder howitzer, two 32 pounder guns, an 8 inch howitzer, an 8 inch columbiad, and a banded rifled piece 42.

(Evans, VI, 1987, 78)

Robert Underwood Johnson, and Clarence Clough Buel, (eds.), *Battles and Leaders of the Civil War*, IV, (Secaucus: Castle Books), 27.

6   L. Cheves McCord: Original captain of the South Carolina Zouaves, died on January 23, 1863 from wounds received at the Second Manassas.

(Simpson, 1977, 448)

Kiss Harry and Robbie for me and give my love to all.[7]
Your affectionate Bro.,
    Elliott

In July 1862 Company H moved north into Virginia and joined its regiment, then a part of Brigadier General John B. Hood's famous Texas Brigade, in time to observe a small action on the Rappahannock River (Hazel River) at Freeman's Ford on August 22, 1862. A fist fight over ears of corn between a Texan and a Federal forager led to a nasty skirmish in the tall corn. The Federals opened fire with an artillery piece which killed Fritz Mathee (Company B), mortally wounded Major D. M. Whaley and J. B. Wilson (Company K), and injured six other men of the 5th Texas.[8]

On August 30, during the second day of the Battle of Second Manassas, the 5th Texas, the 18th Georgia, and the Hampton Legion became separated from the 1st Texas and the 4th Texas. The three regiments in their independent action across Young's Branch scattered the 5th New York (Duryea's Zouaves), inflicting over 80% casualties among the 500 Federals engaged. Henry Brandes (Company H) captured one of the two colors which the Legion took on the field that day.[9] The three regiments then overran Company G, 1st Pennsylvania Artillery which the brigade had fought at Gaines' Mill during the Seven Days' Battles. In capturing the four guns, they mortally wounded Captain Mark Kerns, who commanded the guns and lost many men in the process.

The Legion beat the other two regiments to the field pieces, with Lieutenant Colonel Martin W. Gary claiming that the Legion's colors were the first planted among the battery. Two members of

---

7   Welch came from a large family. In addition to his father, mother and six brothers and sisters, an aunt named Mary (age 50) lived with them.
  Entry for Samuel B. Welch, Charleston County, SC, Census of Population, (National Archives [hereafter cited as NA] Microfilm, roll 1216, 215), Records of the Census, 1860, NA, South Carolina.

8   J. B. Polley, *Hood's Texas Brigade* (Dayton, OH: Morningside Books, 1976), 74-75.
  Simpson maintains that the incident occurred on August 22 and that the casualties were incurred on August 21 in fording the Rappahannock. Unfortunately he did not explain why his information conflicted with Polley's account.
  Harold B. Simpson, *Hood's Texas Brigade: Lee's Grenadier Guard* (Dallas, TX: Alcor Publishing Co., 1983), 136-138.

9   Gary mistakenly cited Brandes as a member of Company C.
  (Polley, 1976, 100)

Company C and Captain Cheves McCord's Company H turned the guns on the Federals and held the position until relieved by Nathan Evans' South Carolina brigade.

The fighting cost Company H dearly. Captain McCord went down with three wounds. 1st Lieutenant John D. Palmer fell nearby as did 2nd Lieutenant T. A. G. Clarke.[10] Elliott Welch was hit in the left leg but refused to leave the field. At least 10 others were wounded, one of whom was also captured, and two were killed.[11] The regiment suffered heavily. By the time it reached Sharpsburg on September 16, only 77 officers and men remained in the ranks. In the following letter describing the regiment's brief actions at Fox's Gap on South Mountain, Maryland (September 14) and in the infamous Cornfield of Antietam on September 17, Elliott Welch explained how the battalion lost 55 of those men in killed and wounded.[12] In the letter which follows his account of the Battle of Antietam he described his arduous walk through the Shenandoah Valley to reach the hospitals in Richmond, Virginia.

Winchester, Va.

[Monday] Sept. 22nd 1862

My dear Parents,

Doubtless you have seen by the papers that I am among the wounded of the battle fought in Maryland. I believe I wrote you last just before crossing the Potomac into Maryland. We travelled on and were near Hagerstown, when we learned of the approach of the enemy. As they were between the river & ourselves we had to meet them.

Sunday, the 14th, we marched back and filed into a cross road [at Boonsboro, Maryland] where one of our batteries was firing on the Yankees but a battery of the enemy's obtained our range & we had to move. Our next position was at the foot of a steep mountain [South Mountain], and then we had to march to the top. A call was then made for 3 volunteer skirmishers & [Henry]

---

10   (*Ibid.*, 87-111)
     (Simpson, 1983, 134-158)

11   (Simpson, 1977, 449-453)

12   (Polley, 1976, 121)

Brandes, [George B.] Gelling & I stept out.[13] Under one of the Lts. we pushed ahead and on reaching the crest of the mountain we saw a line of blue coats [51st Pennsylvania] not 30 yards from us. Fortunately they did not see us, so taking deliberate aim we fired & withdrew; it had the effect of astonishing them and as soon as possible they fired upon us in return, doing no damage, however. Not being ranked [in line of battle] we [four] lay down & the Yanks fired over us.[14] During the night we retired & I was nearly captured, being only a qtr. of a mile off asleep.

I escaped and Monday & Tuesday we were in line of battle. Tuesday night we were under a terrific fire of shot & shell, but only a few were wounded, among them [Henry] Brandes.[15] His wound is not serious but is quite painful.

Wednesday, the 17th, the day opened with a hail storm of shell, grape & canister shot and until 8 a.m. we had to submit to it, but we heard the order to forward and off we went. Coming to a fence we had to climb it and then additionally expose ourselves but once over and like a hurricane we swept over the land. I stood near the flag and saw it fall but being hard at work loading I did not pick it up though it was raised by a color corporal [James E. Estes, Company F] before I was ready.[16] Seeing it floating again I pressed on.

The first gun I had wouldn't go off; throwing it down I found another when, like the first, [it] wouldn't shoot so I had to get a third, which [at] last fired well. After firing five or six shots I fell,

---

13   Henry Brandes: Company H, Hampton Legion, was wounded in the abdomen on September 16. 1862.

George B. Gelling: Company H, Hampton Legion, was wounded on September 17, 1862. (Simpson, 1977, 449, 450)

14   Seconds before this incident, a member of the 35th Massachusetts accidentally shot Major General Jesse Reno (IX Corps, commander). Welch and his men fired into the 51st Pennsylvania which was between the Confederates and the 35th Massachusetts, which returned fire through and over the New Yorkers. These are the shots which sailed over the four South Carolinians.

John M. Priest, *Before Antietam: The Battle for South Mountain*, (Shippensburg: White Mane Publishing Co., Inc., 1992), 218.

15   The Hampton Legion was on the southern side of "The Cornfield."

John M. Priest, *Antietam: The Soldiers' Battle*, (Shippensburg: White Mane Publishing Co., Inc., 1989), 21.

16   Herod Wilson, Company F, went down with the colors first. (Polley, 1976, 126-127)

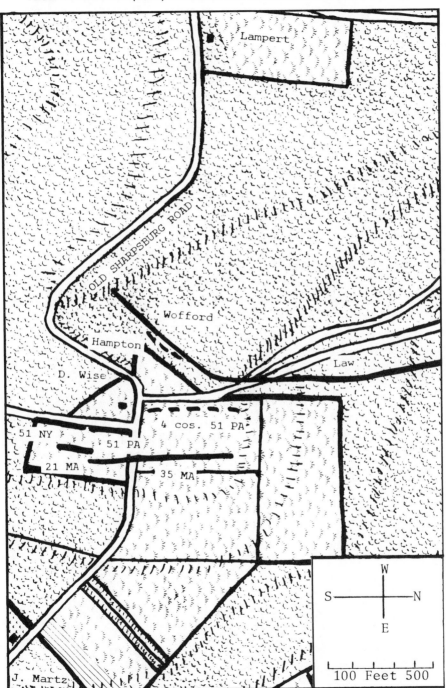

Lampert

OLD SHARPSBURG ROAD

Wofford

Hampton

Law

D. Wise

51 NY

4 cos. 51 PA

51 PA

21 MA

35 MA

J. Martz

W

S ——— N

E

100 Feet 500

Fox's Gap — September 14, 1862. Hood's division closes in on Hartranft's brigade.

doubled up & lay insensible for awhile; as soon as my senses returned I felt a queer sensation on my head & found my right eye closed & ear full of blood & a pool of blood by my side; my rifle was thrown one way & hat another. Picking up my cap it bore no trace of a cut on the outside but the inside was much torn. It is really a mercy I was not torn to pieces for it appeared I never saw rain fall faster than the bullets did around us.

I fired every shot at the U.S. flags and as fast as [they were] raised they fell again.[17] We rushed to within 50 or 60 yards of their battery and the grape & canister tore immense holes through our ranks.[18] Our reinforcements did not come up, but theirs did & on both flanks and in front we had one continued sheet of flame. All around me the bullets whistled and from a battery far on our right the shells burst upon us. A piece of shell struck me and knocked me stupid.

Never have I seen men fall so fast and thick and in about one hour's time our whole division was almost annihilated. The order was given for us to retreat and slowly, sullenly we fell back but as soon as our reinforcements arrived we forwarded up again and drove them back. As an evidence of that fire we had six color bearers shot down: the Major [J. Hervey Dingle] was killed holding them up and the others were wounded.[19]

I had to get off the field the best way I could and after hunting for several hours found the hospital where I had my head dressed. We were then sent across the Potomac to Shepherdstown [Virginia] where we almost starved but for the kindness of a lady and [a] gentleman whom we asked to cook a little meat for us; not content with cooking the meat she had some nice bread and

---

17   The colors belonged to the 2nd Wisconsin and the 6th Wisconsin regiments as they fled from the field.
(Priest, 1989, 56)

18   The Hampton Legion engaged Lieutenant James Stewart's advanced portion of Company B, 4th U.S. Artillery in the field west of the Cornfield.
(Ibid.)

19   J. Hervey Dingle, having been elected 1st lieutenant in Company C on April 25, 1862, had not been officially promoted to the rank of major at the time of his death.
Besides J. H. Dingle, Herod Wilson, and James E. Estes, who died, the Federals wounded 2nd Corporal Christopher P. Poppenheim (Company A), Marion Walton (Company B), and a third, unidentified member of the color guard.
(Simpson, 1977, 403, 413, 416)
(Polley, 1976, 126-127)

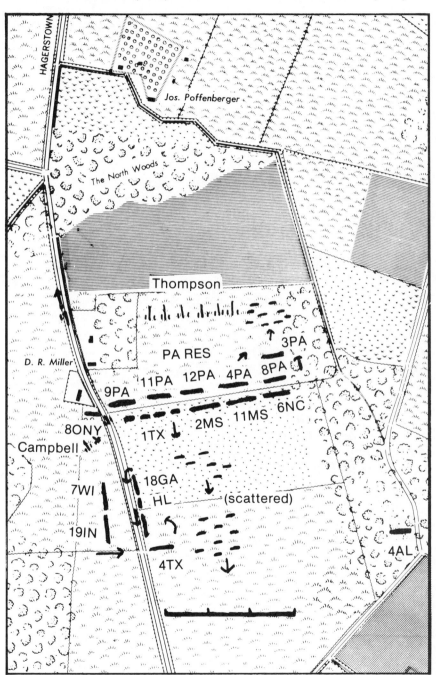

7:00 A.M. — 7:20 A.M., SEPTEMBER 17, 1862
The decimation of the Texas Brigade in the Cornfield.

preserves set out for us. On leaving we were requested to call again and we did so until orders for moving to this town came. Enclosed are the names of our kind friends Mr. [John] & Mrs. [Sallie] Criswell.[20] *Save the card for me.*

Winchester is quite a nice town and the people are very kind to us. In the hospital our accommodations are very scant and provisions are rather scarce but some better arrangements will be made in a day or two for us. So many soldiers have passed through the various towns in Va. & Md. that the wounded can not buy anything but we manage now & then to get something.

Our Army retreated from Maryland but has again crossed into it. The Yankees did not get much of a victory. With nearly six times our force they had us almost entirely surrounded but we drove them back on the left & centre and slept on the field.[21]

I should like to see a copy of the telegraphic news; if you can get it please send it in a letter. Direct as formerly to Richmond. I have [not] rec'd a letter from home since early in August, but the movements of the army are so varied that we do not know one day where we shall be the next. I love the looks of Maryland and it was a pity to desolate such a beautiful country. After we left Frederick City [on the National Pike] we marched up the valley and climbed the Blue Ridge Mts. [at Turner's Gap] from the top of which we had a magnificent view of the vale for miles. Such a sight, I never saw in any State. The beauty of the scenery charmed me & if I live till after the War I should like to have a farm & settle down there.

We obtained a quantity of apples of the finest sort, which were very nice indeed; we miss them now.

I am anxious to hear something of Geo. [Gelling], have not seen anything of him or the Legion since I was wounded. I am quite well, and suffer from my head only at night. The wound is more than an inch long, on the scalp, and just touching the bone. I am

---

20   John was around 41 years of age and Sallie was about 40.
Entry for John Criswell, Jefferson County, VA, Census of Population (NA Microfilm, roll 1335, 946) Records of the Census, 1860, NA, Virginia.

21   The incident Welch referred to is the Battle of Shepherdstown, September 20, 1862. A. P. Hill's Confederate division forced a division of the Fifth Corps across the Potomac River at Boteler's Ford.
(Johnson and Buel, II, 672-673)

thankful my life is spared, for surely it seems no one ever had a more narrow escape than myself. My spirits are up at high water mark.

Give my love to Sammie, Carrie, Henry, Theo. & kiss Robbie for me. My love to Aunt Emily, Uncle William & family as well as Mr. & Mrs. M. Inness.[22] Write whenever you have a chance & I shall do the same. God bless you my dear parents is my daily pray.

Yr. Affectionate Son
Elliott
Excuse errors & c.

Richmond, Va.
[Friday] October 3rd 1862

My dear Parents:

(I forgot to enclose Mr. & Mrs. Criswell's card in my last [letter] but I do so this time.)

I wrote you last from Winchester where we remained in the Hospital till Wednesday the 24th ult. when I concluded to go to Staunton, [Virginia] hoping to obtain a furlough or leave to visit home. In company with one of our wounded men I started and walked 18 miles that day. We passed through several towns, one of which — Newtown — contains many patriotic men & women; it is in the valley of the Shenandoah & is a pretty place. At the door of one of the houses stood a young lady & her mother, who inquired if we had breakfasted & upon learning that he had not, they invited us in & gave us some bread & butter & some delightful biscuit; after eating they dressed our wounds and as there was a little rain just then we staid a while & had a very pleasant chat. Proceeding on, we passed Strasburg in the afternoon, but not seeing any inviting place we left it and intended sleeping on the banks

---

22   Welch refers to Emily Welch, age 42, William H. Welch, age 40 (a bookbinder from Charleston), and their 4 children — Edgar (age 18), Mary (age 17), Allen (age 6), and Lillie (age 4).

Sammie refers to Samuel B. Welch (age 15) and Carrie is Caroline W. Welch (age 13), Welch's brother and sister. I could not identify Theo. who was probably born after 1860.

Charles A. Inness lived in Charleston, Ward 4.

Entries for Samuel and William Welch, and Charles A. Inness, Charleston County, SC, Census of Population, (NA Microfilm, roll 1216, 215, 362, 416), Records of the Census, 1860, South Carolina.

of the river Shenandoah. Seeing a man on the opposite bank I inquired if he could sell me a chicken, sending up to ascertain he asked if I wouldn't come over & stay all night. Of course, we couldn't refuse such a kind offer, and crossing the stream in a boat, we were soon inside of a comfortable farm house and made friends with the good lady. We got the <u>chicken</u>; *it was fried, with cream sauce, a savory dish, this with green corn boiled in milk, delightful biscuit, honey & etc., etc., comprised our supper. About 9 o'clock we went to bed & slept in a bed!!! think of that.*

The next morning [September 25] we eat a nice, hearty breakfast & the old lady made up a package of rolls, apples & peaches for us before leaving and then would not accept a cent of pay. We gave her our names, regt. & State and rec'd an invitation to call on our return. Thursday night we lay down on the ground to rest. Friday [September 26] on a floor. Saturday [September 27] afternoon, seeing two little boys driving a light Jersey wagon I asked and obtained permission to ride a few miles. The little chaps, on learning we had no place to stop at, at night asked us to their house and as it is a soldier's policy to refuse nothing that will benefit him I was not long deciding what to do. We went and found the boys' mother — an elderly lady — a very nice person indeed. She welcomed us warmly and had a long conversation with us. There were some young ladies in the house and they came down & joined in the talk. Walking in the garden we got some peaches, which though good were not as fine as our S.C. ones. After supper we saw the whole family — 3 boys & 5 girls. Together we had a general war talk and then retired.

The following day being Sunday [September 28], the old lady requested us to stay and go with the family to church. We consented to remain though I felt rather ashamed of myself for my shoes were just held on by the strings — almost barefooted — my old Georgia plains trousers, which have not been washed for two months, with two bullet holes through it & so torn that they looked ridiculous; a dirty shirt and all together making a rough appearance. But, dear parents, when I considered how long I had been without hearing the word of God preached I determined to go regardless of looks. At 11 o'clock the service commenced and I was much pleased with the sermon. The text was "And be doers of the word and not hearers only, deceiving yourselves."

When I told Mrs. [Elizabeth F. M.] Dovel — for that is the lady's name — about my parents, she said she knew they would be glad to hear I had an opportunity to hear a sermon.[23] In the afternoon a number of young ladies came to the house and in true country style, regardless of the conventionalities of society, they laughed and talked with us like old friends. In the apple orchard we gathered and exchanged fruit and passed a pleasant time together.

Monday morning [September 29] we started on a tramp again and when a couple of miles off were overtaken by the wagon with two of the young ladies & the two youngsters. With them we rode several miles to a small village called Mt. Sidney. There we parted & were requested to stop again whenever we passed through the valley. Late in the afternoon we reached Staunton and found it a good sized town, but on inquiring prices found them exorbitantly high. We put up at a hotel, which is used as a hospital and in a corner room and enjoyed ourselves finally.

Tuesday morning [September 30] we took the train and by night we reached Richmond, and were put into a very nice Hospital where we remained 24 hours and then came here to stay till sufficiently well to go back to the Legion. Our present domicile is the Masonic Hall; hospital "21," where we are better fed and cared for than anywhere we have yet been. At Winchester, we rec'd a small pc. of bread & meat for breakfast, the same for dinner, with the addition of a mouthful of soup; no supper was allowed. I should have died for starvation at that rate. Winchester is 20 miles from Shepherdstown and Staunton 92 from W. that beside the 8 or 9 we walked in Md. after the battle made a little pleasure trip of about 130 miles, that with 136 miles on the R.R. makes quite a long distance we have travelled since being wounded.

The valley in Md. is really a lovely spot and I must give you a description of it. We passed through a good sized town called Frederick City, from there we visited Middletown and then got into the mountains from which, at an elevation of 400 or 500 feet

23   Elizabeth F. M. Dovel (age 36) lost her husband, David, between 1860-1862. The strain must have aged her considerably. In his letter home Welch said she had 5 boys and 3 girls, which I attribute to a writing error. The children were: Mary S. (age 18), William T. (age 17), Rebecca E. (age 15), Viola E. (age 13), Lewis C. (age 12), Emma F. (age 10), Virgil C. (age 6), and Laura E. (age 4).

Entry for David Dovel, Page County, VA, Census of Population (NA Microfilm, roll 1369, 731) Records of the Census, 1860, NA, Virginia.

we looked back on the valley which is surrounded by the mountains. Below us were the beautiful farm houses & the large granaries & barns; the farms [are] laid out so regularly; the corn [is] planted in rows so even that they seem like lines drawn on paper; the orchard with peaches, apples, pears, quinces & c.; the dairies and cattle; the elegant gardens, all formed a most lovely landscape view. There, and in the northern part of Va. every farmer seems anxious to have a fine barn and each one tries to out vie the other in size & looks. Many of the houses are built of pieces of stone, of various sizes & colors, which make on the whole a fine appearance. Every one looks so cozy, comfortable & homelike that I was quite captivated and vastly preferred the pleasures & quiet of such a life, to the rough wild life of a soldier. As I turned from the peaceful view I thought what a sin it would be to devastate that quiet spot by a battle. Hardly a week elapsed before "Red ruin ruled triumphantly": blood flowed as freely as water and all to no avail. We hadn't sufficient troops or we should have utterly ruined the Federal hopes.

And now the valley of Va. walking along the turnpike road the best in the State — you see the Blue Ridge Mts. on the one hand and on the other Shenandoah ridge [and] between runs the river, which taking a winding course is like a silver thread in places, while in other [places] it rushes & boils over the rocks forming a series of beautiful cascades. On the hilltops, can be seen the clouds settling in great scraps, as it were, and from the distance the Mountains seem to wear an eternal look of blue & green. In some places, on the sides can be seen some elegant dwellings, nice farms & houses and everything so tempting that I could just stop & spend the balance of my days amongst them.

And then, after getting on the trains about 20 miles from Staunton, and passing through a tunnel, more than a mile long, you suddenly emerge with daylight, the scene, far, far below is almost like a paradise. From the elevated point of the R.R. you can see the hills jutting out & standing in bold relief the skies and then it appears to be a mile down to the houses below. At once there is a scene, wild, grand & sublime but as the train nears the Capital the cultivation seems less careful and a great want of attention & care becomes visible. I wish the times were peaceful and you all

14

could come of it and enjoy the lovely views & fresh mountain air that we have. When passing through the valley of Va. we had a pleasant time & lived high, without expense, everyone displaying a disposition to do everything in their power for the soldiers, particularly the sick & wounded.

Now to let you know about myself, I am nearly barefooted, ragged dirty & penniless but we have a kind Surgeon who attends to our department & he is preparing to draw shoes, clothing & our money, so I shall require no assistance from home — in fact it would be almost impossible for me to hear from you anyhow. I have not heard from home since Sammie wrote me about Grandma's death. Perhaps the letters have gone on to the Legion who are now resting at Winchester — if so I shall get them for I expect to return in the course of two or three weeks.

My head is rapidly getting well and healing up. Sometimes the pain is rather great but it does not last very long. I should like to have had a furlough but men are needed in the Valley & I must be at my post. I am in good health & spirits.

Give my love to Willie when you write him, to Sammie & Carrie, Henry & Theo. Kiss Robbie for me, My love to Uncle W., Aunt E. & family, Mr. & Mrs. Cook, Cousin Laura & family, Mr. & Mrs. W. & Miss Hellen & all friends.[24]

God bless you and preserve you from harm is the constant prayer of Your Affectionate Son.

Elliott

On November 18, 1862, as the result of the reorganization of the Army of Northern Virginia, the Hampton Legion transferred into Brigadier General Micah Jenkins' South Carolina Brigade (2nd Rifles, 1st, 5th, 6th regiments, and Palmetto Sharpshooters).[25] Elliott Welch rejoined his regiment on December 1.[26] Less than two weeks later, on December 13, 1862, the Legion with its brigade took part in the Battle of Fredericksburg. General James Longstreet

---

24   I was unable to locate these individuals in the Census records. Welch did not provide enough data to identify them.

25   (Simpson, 1983, 194)

26   (Simpson, 1977, 448)

detached the brigade from Major General George E. Pickett's division and placed it in the sunken road with Brigadier General Robert Ransom's division in the defense of Marye's Heights. (The division lost 54 men during the entire day.)

On January 2. 1863 Elliott received an appointment as the 2nd sergeant of Company H. Within thirty days he won the election as junior 2nd lieutenant. The following letter represents Elliott Welch's only extant correspondence for 1863. He wrote it two weeks before Longstreet's Corps moved south to Petersburg.

> *Legion's Camp near Fredericksburg*
> *[Sunday] February 1st 1863*

My dear Parents:

At last your oldest boy is an officer in the Army. I am now a Lieut. in the Hampton Legion, though [I] cannot take my place in the line of officers till my examination comes off, which as yet I cannot ascertain when it will occur. I have some misgivings as to the result & fear I am not competent, but hope by patient study to be able to pass the test, but hope by patient study to be able to pass the ordeal safely. Yesterday morning [Saturday, January 31], Capt. [John D.] Palmer called me and told me it was the desire of himself as well as [of] the Col. [Martin W. Gary] that I should be elected & on ascertaining that [Private] Donald [J.] Auld [Company H] wouldn't run I decided to risk my chance.[27] By 12½ o'clock the election was over. I had two opponents one of whom rec'd two votes, the other seventeen; I rec'd twenty four of forty three polled. Col. Gary has little or no use for either [1st Lieutenant Thomas A. G.] Clarke or [2nd Lieutenant William G.] Gardner and told Palmer that he wanted to see me in.[28] After the election, Lt.

---

27   John D. Palmer, the original 1st lieutenant of Company H, was wounded at 2nd Manassas on August 30, 1862 and became the captain of the company on January 23, 1863.

Martin W. Gary began his long career with the Legion as the captain of Company B. On June 16, 1862 he became the lieutenant colonel and by August 25, 1862 he was the colonel of the Legion.

Donald J. Auld, Company H, who was reduced to the ranks with Welch earlier in 1862, rose to the rank of 2nd sergeant before the end of the war.

(Simpson, 1977, 398, 448, 449)

28   T. A. G. Clarke, the original 1st lieutenant of Company H, became the 1st lieutenant on April 12, 1862. Wounded on August 30, 1862 at 2nd Manassas, he returned to the regiment as 1st lieutenant in time for the Knoxville Campaign.

William G. Gardner started the war as a private in Company H. He won the election to the

Col. [Thomas M.] Logan sent for me, shook my hands and con-gratulated me upon my rise and told me he depended on Palmer & myself to keep the company up.[29] *I believe I have the confidence of both [of] our Field Officers and will endeavor to prove myself worthy of it. Palmer thinks both Clarke & Gardner will be dished and in the event of my standing the severe pressure I may be 2nd or 1st Lieut. I sincerely hope the examination will not prove to me in reality [to be] the terrible trial [which] it seems to be in the ideal.*

If you have a chance to send anything please send me my "Hardee" and "School of the Guides."[30] *Should no other oppor-tunity offer [itself] send the "Guides" book by mail. I'll send to Rich-mond for a copy of the "Army Regulations." If Father [Samuel B. Welch] sees a chance I wish he'd inquire [about] the price of [a] Confederate coat and sword. The latter can be purchased in Rich-mond for $28.00 at the Ordnance Office. The coat out here costs about $75.00 or $100.00 a heavy sum certainly, but [it] can't be helped. The coat I shall use for dress & my jacket will answer for all marching or rough purposes. The sash which I left [at] home will come in very well, though such things are rarely used in the Army nowadays, so mine may rest at home. a trophy of Manassas.*

Palmer went home today, much to my regret, for the prin-cipal part of the affair devolves upon me. Clarke, I think, is not very anxious to get back, though the fact of his being 1st Lieut. may hasten his return. A much longer delay and [his] name will be dropped from the regimental roll. We have lost all faith in him and he had better hasten himself to save his position.

[3rd Sergeant E. J.] Dumaresa [Company H] was appointed Orderly [1st Sergeant] and [Private P. E.] DeCamps 2nd Sergt. last

---

2nd lieutenancy on October 2, 1862 and rose to acting 1st lieutenant on January 23, 1863 while Clarke was on convalescence furlough.

Elliott Welch received his appointment to acting 2nd lieutenant on January 31, 1863 to serve in Gardner's place who in turn assumed Clarke's post.

(*Ibid.*, 448)

29   Thomas M. Logan, by the age of 23, had risen from the captaincy of Company A, Hampton Legion to lieutenant colonel on December 13, 1862. He finished the war as a brigadier general.

(*Ibid.*, 398)

30   They were two of the more popular drill manuals used by both armies to train their men.

night, the 3rd is still vacant and George [Gelling] will get it if he returns.[31] I hope he will be with us ere long.[32]

Last Tuesday [January 27] I rec'd a letter from Miss Hellen, the following day one from Miss Hill and another from Willie and Friday one from home; yesterday I rec'd another from you announcing the sad intelligence of Mr. Cook's death. Tell Cousin Mary [Welch] I sympathize with her great affliction.[33] I am glad however he left his affairs in a prospering state, & his wife free of trouble.

I shall see to the affairs of Mr. Sanders' requests & write him as soon as possible.[34] Capt. Palmer took some $38.50 for him & I shall see the Quartermaster & ascertain if I can get the balance due the Corporal [H. J. Sanders].

My throat is much better, thanks to Miss Hill's kindness — she sent me some red peppers & directions to make a gargle. I am now quite well.

Saturday [January 31] we rec'd the intelligence of the resignation of five Yankee Generals. I hope they will all do likewise. The stirring news of Lt. Col. [Joseph A.] Yates' [1st South Carolina Artillery] capturing a gunboat in the Stono [River] was heard.[35] Yesterday a telegram announcing the raising of the Charleston Blockade came, shouts of joy greeted it, hats were thrown in the air and everybody, in our brigade especially was in a high state of excitement and glee at the success. Did [Commodore Duncan N.] In-

---

31   E. J. Dumaresa, a former private in Company H, became the 3rd sergeant during the summer of 1862. He remained the 1st sergeant from February 1, 1863 until he was reduced to the ranks in the Fall of 1864. He finished the war as the company's 2nd sergeant.
P. E. DeCamps enlisted as a private in Company H. He remained 2nd sergeant until he was discharged on June 30, 1863 with heart trouble.
(Simpson, 1977, 449)

32   Gelling returned to the regiment and became the 3rd sergeant. On February 19, 1864, he transferred to Company C 27th South Carolina.
(*Ibid.*)

33   Willie is William Hawkins Welch, Elliott's 17 year old brother.
I could not identify Miss Hill or Mr. Cook in the census of 1860.

34   His son, Corporal A. J. Sanders, Company H, who was wounded on August 30, 1862, died from his wounds on January 5, 1863.
(Simpson, 1977, 449)

35   Lieutenant Colonel Yates and his volunteers captured the gunboat "Isaac Smith" on January 30, 1863. The Confederates captured 11 officers and 108 men in the affair and converted the boat to their own use as the "Stono."
(Johnson and Buel, IV, 7-8)

graham command?[36] *It is three cheers for him and those under him. We look for today's papers with anxiety.*

Since my last [letter], we had a terrible snow storm and the earth was covered with five or six inches of snow. If I have time & space in my next [letter] I'll give you an account of a severe battle between our Brigade & Law's Alabama Brigade in which we beat and drove them through their camp. The snow fight was a grand affair & I must try to give you a description of it.[37]

Give my love to all enquiring friends, whom I have no time to enumerate.

Please enquire the price of a black felt hat which I should have, or else an Infantry officer's cap. Write soon and God bless you all is the earnest prayer of Your Affectionate Son.

Excuse haste & errors.   *Elliott*

On February 15, Major General George E. Pickett's Division, to which the Hampton Legion belonged, left the Massaponax River for Richmond. The rest of the Corps followed two days later. Seven days after that [February 22, 1863], after several days of hard marching in driving snow and sleet, Longstreet's men entered the capital of the Confederacy to the cheers of the local citizenry. The weary veterans of Hood's and Pickett's divisions remained in the vicinity of Richmond until April when they moved southeast toward Suffolk to thwart a Federal thrust from the coast.[38] Pickett's division formed the right wing of a fifteen mile, tenuously held front against a stalled Federal advance and cautious gunboats in the Nansemond River.

Between mid-April and May 2, Pickett's and Hood's men scoured the farms around the Blackwater River. The local farmers, who had been selling goods to the Federals at inflated prices

---

36 Ingraham, on board the ram "Palmetto State" with the ram "Chicora" broke through the Federal blockade on January 31, 1863. They captured the "Mercidita" and the "Keystone State," disabled the "Quaker City," and chased off two more vessels.
(*Ibid.*, 6-7)

37 On January 29, 1863, while camped along the Massaponax River south of Richmond, the Texas Brigade began a snowball fight which evolved into a full scale battle. With banners flying, bugle blaring. and drums rolling the entire corps apparently became involved in the fighting.
(Simpson, 1983, 205-207)

38 (Simpson, 1983, 213, 224-225)

resented being paid for their meat and grain in deflated Confederate currency. They hated the Confederate infantry even more for "requisitioning" their horses and wagons to haul the provisions away.[39] The Hampton Legion as part of Jenkins' brigade retired with the rest of Longstreet's corps on May 3rd toward Richmond but did not proceed north toward the Army of Northern Virginia along the Rapidan River.[40] The brigade remained in the vicinity of Richmond and Petersburg through the early fall of that year, thereby missing Chancellorsville and (more fortunately) Gettysburg.[41]

In September Jenkins' brigade was transferred to Hood's division, just before Longstreet's corps moved south into Tennessee. At Chickamauga (September 20, 1863) the Federals captured one man from Welch's company — 1st Corporal J. M. Curtis.[42] The Legion actively participated in the action at Will's Valley (Lookout Mountain, Tennessee) on October 28, 1863, where Company H lost at least ten men — killed, wounded and missing.[43]

Between November 17-29, Welch saw service at the siege of Knoxville during which time his company suffered no casualties. The Legion continued to shift about East Tennessee with Longstreet's corps, taking part in minor affairs at Bean's Station (December 19, 1863) and Dandridge (January 15-17, 1864). 1st Lieutenant T. A. G. Clarke, senior officer of Welch's company died in a skirmish there on January 17. His second in command, 2nd Lieutenant William G. Gardner went down seriously wounded on the same day. They were the last members of Company H lost in the Tennessee Campaign.[44]

---

39   (*Ibid.*, 224-243)

40   (*Ibid.*, 233)

41   Company H lost 4th Sergeant M. P. Dannelly in the trenches that Fall. (Simpson, 1977, 449)

42   (*Ibid.*, 449)

43   Killed: B. J. Bars and W.H. Keller.
     Wounded: George B. Gelling, D. W. Bars, H. D. Bolen, C. A. Gregory, E. Hughes and
          H. E. Turner.
     Wounded and Captured: J.M. Garrick
     Captured: W. C. Hutto
(*Ibid.*, 449-452)

44   (*Ibid.*, 448)

Chapter Two

FROM TENNESSEE (1863)
TO THE JAMES RIVER (1864)

From this point on, Elliott Welch's letters become self explanatory and more frequent.

In the mind as usual.
Legion's Bivouac, near Strawberry Plains [Tenn.].[1]
[Sunday] February 14th 1864

Dear Mother

A month ago day before yesterday was my birthday since which time I've written & sent of several letters to you and have not rec'd one in reply, notwithstanding, the trains have been running up to our very camps for over a week and I rec'd a letter this morning from Ga. dated Feby 7th. Is anything the matter, or have my letters failed to come thro' by some mistake? Annie's last was dated 24th ulto. & I should have had one on the 31st unless she was prevented [from] writing by some accident or other; however I look daily for a whole batch and then well, I'll answer them as soon as possible.

The box you sent last Nov. came to hand [the] day before yesterday. The potatoes were, of course, all spoiled,; the biscuit and bread were molded thro'; the rice had turned green, affected by the potatoes. The tea was totally ruined and if sugar had been there it was now lost. A portion of the bacon was tainted, but [I] managed to make use of it, as well as the rice, soda & colic

---

1   Strawberry Plains is about ten miles northeast of Knoxville near the Smokey Mountains.

21

medicine, which I suppose it is. All else was worthless. It was a great disappointment to me, but I am used to such things now. Many thanks for the box.

Yesterday [February 13] we left our camp at New Market & I had to leave my young lady friend, who fixed up my haversack so nicely. Great pity!

I suppose you've seen in some of my letters that I am in command of the company.[2] I am getting on very well indeed. Occasionally I get a few obstreperous cases, but [I] soon settle them by a mild, but firm disposition of their cases. At Inspection this morning a man named [W. A.] Walker, whom I had shown some favors, by allowing him to go scouting & [he] wanted to have his own way & being a quite a braggart makes some believe him a great man; the force of examplement [goes] a considerable way, so forming the company I gave them a "Say," telling them what were their duties & what I expected of them.[3] From this time out I anticipate no difficulty whatever as all understand distinctly the course I shall pursue.

Some time ago I should have declined the Captaincy of the company, doubting my ability to discharge my duties but now I have more confidence in myself, and tho' it sounds boastful, it is truly the case, the affairs of this company were never in a better state. Now, its interests [are] better cared for.

I wrote you about breaking my sword, I believe and also having obtained a pair of yellow brogans, quite gay ornaments for a well furnished parlor, but I am proud of them after trudging barefooted for over two months.

---

2   Company H was in a real mess. Captain John Palmer, who was still on convalescent leave from 2nd Manassas, did not command the company. 1st Lieutenant Thomas Clarke, acting captain, had died in battle on January 17, 1864 at Dandridge, Tennessee. 2nd Lieutenant William G. Gardner, who fell wounded the same day, after Clarke's death, found himself successively promoted on paper to acting 1st lieutenant then captain. 2nd Sergeant Elliott Welch, as acting 2nd lieutenant, was promoted on January 17, 1864 to 1st lieutenant and company command.

The Confederate army did not date the promotions (commissions) and musters of its regimental officers separately as the Federal service did. Promotion could be interpreted as a field promotion and therefore temporary. The commission and the mustering in secured the rank and the pay scale for the individual officer.

(Simpson, 1977, 448)

(Evans, VI, 1987, 903)

3   (Simpson, 1977, 452)

I don't think I told you about Captain [James R.] Hagood (brother of the Gen.) of the 1st [South Carolina] Regt. of our brigade and only 20 years of age was appointed Col. of the regiment over five or six Capt., the Maj., & Lt. Col. It was thro' the instrumentality of his brother [Brigadier General Johnson Hagood] & "Sinks" that he need[s] the appointment. Being the only Col. present he commanded the brigade — quite a rise for a Col. in three weeks, from commanding a company to that of six <u>*regiments*</u>.[4]

Some of my company went to chat with him & speak then disparagingly of the Col.' talents. I wonder if I shall ever be a Col. — hope so if the war has to last long enough.

Willie B. Hughes [Company A] is at Columbia and has written Frank [Hughes, Company A] that he is recommended for discharge [for] having that terrible complaint, consumption.[5] He states that he has at last found the Savior — Oh, that I could so likewise!

We have come down here, toward Knoxville about 10 miles [to the northeast] and are gradually inching on to that Yankee stronghold and as orders have come I send all extra baggage to the rear. I judge another "on to Knoxville" is contemplated, and I hope a more successful one than the last.[6]

Isn't it too bad that even Sunday cannot be had as a day of rest. I had to stop my letter very unceremoniously and finish up the pay rolls this afternoon so the poor fellows could get some money, and there's no Knowing when we shall move.

---

4   James R. Hagood became the youngest colonel in the Army of Northern Virginia. He died in a train accident after the war.

James R. Hagood, "Memoirs of the First South Carolina Regiment of the Volunteer Infantry in the Confederate War for Independence from April 12, 1861 to April 10, 1865," typed manuscript, The South Carolina Library, December, 1928, Foreword.

5   William B. Hughes was wounded at Second Manassas on August 30, 1862. On February 28, 1863, he purchased a substitute which exempted him from further military service.

Frank P. Hughes, the original sergeant major of the Hampton Legion, received a discharge with a disability in April 1862. He reenlisted as a private in company A in November 1862 and served with the regiment until he died on October 14, 1864.

(Simpson, 1977, 401 and 405)

6   For a detailed accounting of the fighting around Knoxville refer to *Battles and Leaders of the Civil War*, III, 731-751.

Welch correctly surmised that the corps was on a second move to Knoxville. Five days after Welch wrote his letter, James Longstreet called off the maneuver when the Confederate government in Richmond failed to send him needed reinforcements.

James Longstreet, *From Manassas to Appomattox* (NY: DaCapo, 1992), 539.

Don't fail to direct [your letters] to [Lieutenant General James] Longstreet's Corps, E. Tenn.

Has Annie arrived at Timmonsville yet? She told me to direct [my letters] there to her and I wrote last Sunday to her as instructed.

Give my warmest love and Kiss her for me as well as the little ones.

One day during the past week I rec'd two month's pay $160.00 and had to pay a commissary acc't of $118.00. That's the way the money goes out here. Of that amount I paid [acting Captain William G.] Gardner's bill of $40.00 which he had the audacity to tell me to pay on the strength of my indebtedness to him for a coat which he forced me to take almost a year ago and said nothing about my owing him for it till the first of this month.

In my next [letter] I shall send the correspondence relating to it home for preservation. It is decidedly rich. He can't make much off me, tho' I'll pay the debt, as a matter of honor — no court could make me settle it.

Do send me a paper once in a while, you save the little news gleaned from letters. We never hear anything.

We have nothing new out here. The change of camp or the daily routine of camp duty is all we see or know. The ostensible purpose of Longstreet is to capture Knoxville and move on the flank of [Major General Ulysses S.] Grant causing him thereby to "change his base" and allow [General Joseph E.] Johnston [Department commander in Tennessee] to start them. If we could move a heavy force to strike into West. Tenn. thereafter Nashville it would cause Grant to move in a hurry. Once out of E. Tenn. I should advocate L.'s [Longstreet's] advance into Ky. & Lee's "onto Washington" again. Something tells me we shall be successful if we invade Md. once more. Twice we've failed. [We need] another and greater effort. War is a curse but I want the Yanks to realize its horrors in their own boundaries.

Don't let a discouraging word drop or entertain any other than a strong faith. Mine's unshaken in our ultimate success. Our Army is hopeful and the re-enlistment "goes bravely on." Our regiment hasn't taken any action as yet. Co. "H" volunteered for the [duration of the] War from the start, so we are all right.

I rec'd a letter from [Captain John D.] Palmer lately & he wants my opinion about his exchange with Capt. [Henry R.] Lesesne of *the Regular Artillery.*[7] *My consent is absolutely necessary for its consummation & I'll resign before granting it. Lesesne is not an honorable gentleman & I shan't improve by the exchange in any way.*

I must close as it is dark. I can't see the lines. We have no candles & the mail leaves early in the morning. I am in the best health and spirits.

Much love to Father, Willie, Sammie, Mrs. White, & Mrs. Collins & family.[8] *Kiss Annie, Carrie, Harry & Robbie for me. Excuse mistakes. Can't correct them. God bless & preserve you all is my daily prayer.*

Your affectionate Son,

Elliott

In May 1864, during the Wilderness Campaign, the Hampton Legion returned to Columbia, South Carolina to become mounted infantry. Elliott Welch, commanding the horse procurement detachment, did not return with the mounts to his battalion, which was stationed below Richmond until near the end of the month as the next letter from Willie, Elliott's younger brother, indicates. At that time, the Legion joined Colonel Martin W. Gary's cavalry command which consisted of the 7th Georgia and 24th Virginia regiments.[9]

In 1862, while Elliott was away in the Army of Northern Virginia, Willie, then age 17, enlisted in the Rutledge Mounted Rifles and late in the year he saw his first action in a brief engagement at a bridge on the Pocotaligo River in South Carolina. Some time in 1863 the Rutledge Mounted Rifles joined the 7th South Carolina Cavalry and split into companies A and G, with young Welch becoming the 2nd sergeant of Company G. In May 1864,

---

7   As a lieutenant, Lesesne commanded the Cumming's Point Battery at Charleston Harbor. In April 1863 he also commanded a company of regular artillery at Fort Sumter. (Johnson and Buel, IV, 11)

Captain Palmer, who was still at home convalescing from his Second Manassas wound, apparently wanted Lesesne to fill his post in the company over Gardner.

8   The names were too generic to track down among the many which matched them in the 1860 census for South Carolina.

9   (Evans, 1987, 396, 904)

as described in the next letter, Willie's regiment rode north into Virginia to join Gary's brigade near Richmond.[10]

> *Bivouac of [Captain William L.] Trenholm's Squadron*[11]
> *[Company G, 7th South Carolina Cavalry]*[12]
> *Near Richmond, [Saturday] May 21st 1864*

My dear Mother,

We have at last reached Richmond after a Long & tiresome march. Our Scouting party that has been following up the Yanks reached here yesterday evening, after being in the saddle every day since leaving Hillsboro, [North Carolina]. 10 days in all, traveling all day & sometimes in the night. During the whole of that time until yesterday [May 20], we've not had a clear day, raining all the time.[13] *Of course I've been in wet clothes all the time. Two weeks ago today [Saturday, May 7] I changed my clothes & took a wash. I don't know how long it will be before I get any more clean clothes on. Our valises was left at Hillsboro & it will be some days before we get them. Our camp is 3 miles from the city & is situated in a low, marshy piece of woods, with very poor water near. In fact it is white mud diluted with water.*

Last night we rec'd 3 days rations. They consisted of ¾ lb. of bacon & 3 small cupfuls of flour to the man. You should have seen me this morning with my hands in the dough. I think you'd have laughed heartily. It was the first time I ever tried it & to my surprise I succeeded admirably. I cooked 3 breads & they were very nice. I mixed the dough in my plate. — Our horses fare very badly here getting but little corn and no long forage; so we turn them out in a clover field several hours a day.

While on the scout at Lawrenceville [Va.] I formed the acquaintance of several very nice ladies & spent several hours very

---

10   (*Ibid.*, 904)

11   Entry for William L. Trenholm, Roster of Trenholm's Company (NA Microfilm roll 56) NA.

12   This is 2nd Sergeant William Hawkins Welch's first letter home.

13   The weather report from Rendezvous Station, Virginia recorded a 2:00 P.M. temperature of 75 degrees with clear skies.
Resource center, Fredericksburg and Spotsylvania National Battlefield Parks.

pleasantly in their company. On leaving they put up a very nice lunch for me, inviting me to stop & see them if I ever came that way again.

All along our road, (on the scout) we were treated handsomely, the people giving us more than we could eat. I had 3 days rations of flour in my haversack, & I didn't touch it, being fed by the ladies. May God bless & protect them for their kindness to the Soldiers. When we told them we were from So. Ca. our welcome & reception were heartier & more cordial, if such a thing be possible. The Virginians seem to admire the So. Carolinians. Our treatment in passing through No. Ca. was certainly very good, but as soon as we crossed the Virginia line we noticed the difference. Va. is far ahead of even So. Ca. for hospitality.

Had I not been told I would have bet we were in Va. as soon as we reached Clarksville, the first village in the state we passed thro', for the ladies came into the streets & gave us bouquets, & eatables. On our way through, [John] Smythe, [H. T.] Whitney & I fared very well, for we'd go to a house & ask for supper, & we were only once refused, & in no case would the good people accept pay.[14] We'd generally pick out a large house where we thought they could afford to give us supper, & where there were some young ladies. It requires considerable brass, & at first made us feel very awkward & embarrassing, but we soon got over that.

I like the appearance of the country around Richmond very much, but the roads are in terrible condition. The prettiest country we've passed thro' yet was between Charlotte & Salisbury, N.C. It is rolling & it is really a beautiful sight to look at it.

We've been 30 days on the road, excluding our stay at Columbia & Charlotte & altho' I got very tired of riding before the day's march is over, I'd prefer to be on the go all the time to staying at camp. I don't want to stay in this hole another day if I can help it. I'm perfectly disgusted with it.

The enemy are about 10 miles below us in force & our Squadron pickets in their front. Our Regt. is at Drewry's Bluff, & we may go there shortly to join them, but for the present I think we'll remain here for the defence of Richmond against raiding parties.

---

14   Roster of the 7th South Carolina Cavalry, (NA Microfilm, roll 48).

Ask Sammie to get me that tin can for putting paper in, & I'll write him [on] how to send it.

Well I must close now. Give my love to Father, Sammie, Carrie, Ellie, Robbie & Sister Annie & Maggie W. Has Carrie returned from C. yet? Kind regards to Mrs. White, Mrs. Collins & family. Mrs. Wells & the young ladies & Misses Parker & Keith, & Co. & any other friends.[15]

I am well & healthy & in good spirits. Communications between Richmond and the South have been cut off for two weeks, or I would expect a letter or two from you. However write soon & long letters, & I'll write at every opportunity.

May God bless & protect you all is my sincerest prayer.

Your affectionate Son,
Willie

May 22nd [Sunday]. Direct to Trenholm's Squadron Care Army P.O. Richmond, Va.

Yesterday a scouting party of ten men from our Squadron was sent out, & last night they ret'd with two missing, supposed to have been captured. The rest were run [off] by a body of Yankee cavalry. We are to go into [Colonel General Martin W.] Gary's Brigade, & the Hampton Legion being there, Ellie & I will be together.[16] *We expect to go to Hanover Junction soon.*

Willie

We had nothing to Eat. For two days I had no meat, nothing but corn bread, & not enough of that. Yesterday morning we left,

---

15   The names for most of these were too vague to positively identify, however there was a very wealthy P. T. Keith and family living in Ward 4 of Charleston. He was the only Keith in the area and quite possibly was an associate of Mr. Welch. P. T. Keith (age 61) was a Protestant Episcopal minister whose personal property alone was valued at $77,000 in 1860. His family included his wife, Anna (age 60), Madeline (age 34), Susan (age 30), Willis (age 24), Mark (age 23), Anna (age 24), Maria (age 21), Eleanor (age 13), Maggie (age 17), Anne (age 16), Mary (age 14) and Paul (age 12).

The Miss Parker he refers to probably is a member of the F. A. Parker family who lived in the same Charleston Ward as the Welch's. F. A. Ward (age 54) was a professor of history. His family included his wife, Caroline (39), and 6 children: Edison A. (age 24), Anna L. (age 21). F. G. (age 19), Alice L. (age 16), Nancy B. (age 12), and Caroline (age 9).

Entries for P. T. Keith and F. A. Parker, Charleston County, Charleston, SC, Census of Population, (NA Microfilm, roll 1216, 215, 358) Records of the Census, 1860, South Carolina.

16   Gary, who had served with the Legion since First Manassas, had seen action in every campaign.
(Evans, 1987, 395-396)

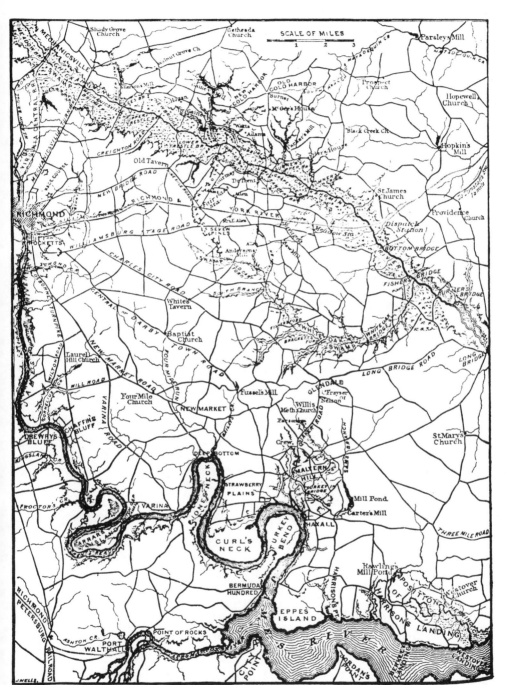

The Chickahominy and the James Rivers.
Battles and Leaders of the Civil War

in the rain for Malvern Hill where we stopped for several hours, & then left again & are now within 2 miles of it. I forgot to mention that the only casualty in the battery was one artillery horse wounded. We have rain & plenty of it last night & day.

[Tuesday] June 7th [1864]

Willie commenced this and as his regt. is ordered off to Malvern Hill to encamp he requested me [Elliott Welch] to finish it for him.

So far as news is concerned, there is a perfect dearth. An occasional gun is all that can be heard along the lines. Our pickets are all comfortably situated and don't wish to be relieved. [Captain John D.] Palmer is still out, so [acting Captain William G.] Gardner is in command & I am at [Commissary Sergeant Donald John] Auld's tent.[17]

Yesterday afternoon [June 6] I obtained permission to go to the regt's camp and returned last night about 10 o'clock. The mail carrier soon after arrived with a letter from Annie dated Charleston June 1st. This morning yours of May 30th came up. Many thanks for remembering me so often. Willie showed me his letter from yourself of a recent date. Yesterday I wrote Annie, having written you from Burkesville, but [I] didn't send it until we reached Richmond. I also wrote George Gelling a long letter, giving him an outline of my trip from S.C.

[A] Report says there's a considerable force of negro soldiers on the opposite side of the Chickahominy, and cavalry, splendidly equipped with excellent uniforms, two pistols, sabre & Sharpes rifle, besides having the best sorts of horses. Oh! if only we could get at them — no prisoners from those Yanks.[18]

I have managed to "flank" an excellent English Sabre, so I'll not be at the expense of buying a sword, the cheapest of which is about $110 in Richmond.[19]

---

17   Auld took part in every major engagement of the regiment except South Mountain. He started the war as 2nd Sergeant of Company H.
(Evans, 1987, 435-436)

18   Welch referred to Brigadier General Edward W. Hinks' division of seven regular army black infantry regiments and the 1st and 2nd U.S. Colored Cavalry.
Under decree of the Confederate government, no quarter in battle referred to any blacks taken prisoner in Federal uniform. Welch, despite his insinuation that he desired revenge upon black troops, when it came to actual combat with them, did not personally carry out his threat.
(Johnson and Buel, IV, 182)

19   In the original letter Welch consistently wrote his $ sign at the end of the number.

FROM TENNESSEE (1863) TO THE JAMES RIVER (1864)

Willie is looking exceedingly well and seems to fancy the Va. life very well indeed. His comrades like himself are very lively, full of mischief. They are pleasantly situated <u>en bivouac</u> on the blood stained field of Malvern Hill. The camping ground we now occupy is literally covered with bones bleaching in the warmth of summer sun.

Our men were all around, and clinging to the skeletons we found around us are fragments of blue cloth, indicating that they are the detested foe. In their cries "On to Richmond" how many of these wretches have been hurled into eternity.

God grant the enemy may soon see how utterly useless it is to attempt our subjugation & soon listen to common sense and reason. Many deserters are coming into our lines at Bottom's Bridge — thoroughly disgusted with their armies, people forlorn. Oh, may it have its weight throughout the length & the width of their land.

We are having cornmeal & bacon — 1 ¼ lbs of the meal & ⅓ lb of the meat — coarse but substantial food.

Tell Annie, Miss Susie Oakes gave me a book of Tennyson's poems while in Columbia & I'll send the Poems.[20] I read my Testament every day & hope & pray for God's blessing upon it. The kind advice & sincerest longings which both of you express for my spiritual welfare shall not be disregarded. Soon, oh very soon, I hope God will change my heart & bring me an humble penitent to his throne of Grace.

Kiss Annie, Robbie & Harry for me. Send much love to Father, Sammie, Carrie & Maggie. Willie poses me in love to all & regards to the Timmonsville folks. Write soon.

May God bless you & spare us all to meet again, if it be His will is my daily prayer.

Your affectionate Son
Elliott

---

20   L. B. Oakes (age 56), a very wealthy broker who lived in Charleston's Ward 4, had a wife and three children living at home with him: wife, Margaret (age 49), Susan (age 21), Ellen (age 17), and Alice (age 11).

Entry for L. B. Oakes, Charleston County, SC, Census of Population, (NA Microfilm, roll, 1216, 336) Records of the Census, 1860, NA, South Carolina.

Camp of the H[ampton] L[egion] w Infantry Chas. City Co.
[Sunday] June 19th 1864

Dear Mother & Sisters

    I have just passed through a week of adventures & a terrible chapter of incidents. Willie tells me he wrote you & has probably given you an outline of our doings. On Sunday night [June 12] the enemy crossed the Chickahominy at Long Bridge & Bradley's Ford driving in [Brigadier General Rufus] Barringer's pickets, and [sent them] scurrying from his line.[21] *On Monday [June 13] at 1 o'clock in the morning our regiment was ordered down the road at 3½ [A.M.].*[22] *I was sent down a road to the right toward our pickets and watch the road. The regiment was with me at [word obliterated] we heard firing in our rear and off we rode. I was sent to notify Col. [Martin W.] Gary of the way the Legion was going. After riding cross country & delivered my orders we reported to the regiment who were out as skirmishers. Taking a rifle I prepared to give them our visitation & how they came on us with a yell.*

    I had seen Willie, [Private John] Smythe & [Private H. T.] Whitney (both Company G, 7th South Carolina Cavalry), shook hands with them & hope we meet soon again. Firing commenced and I saw the enemy charging us. I was in command of the extreme left with five men, held my position till they were within 50 or 60 yards and after the whole line was gone, I fell back and kept near the line. They crowded us, flanked on both sides, there was no alternative for us but to retreat; we fell back to a point three miles from where the action commenced & there I learned of the loss Willie sustained in [that] Smythe and Whitney had been killed. Oh, what a sad thing! The day before the three dined with me & little did I think we should never meet again. Soon after the enemy came up and drove the enemy back and then threw up breastworks at our camping ground. That evening our works were twice assaulted and both attacks very handsomely repulsed.

---

21   Barringer's brigade consisted of 1st, 2nd, 3rd, and 5th North Carolina cavalry regiments. Federal forces referred to this as the action at Long Bridge. Skirmishes also occurred at White House Landing and Bottom's Bridge.

22   This is the action at Riddell's [Riddle's] Shop. There was fighting at White Oak Swamp, White Oak Swamp Bridge, and Charles City Cross Roads.

I went with Willie to the front to see after the bodies of our friends. We were under fire for a while but found it healthy to get away before [they became] very much interested.

During that night the enemy fell back & our regiment pursued them the next morning [June 14].[23] An advance just being required I was sent for to take command & rode within 100 yards of the rear guard before I was aware of it. The guard had been sent out & I was to go & take command; and seeing blue men in front I galloped up, but wasn't shot at. Soon I saw them again, drew up my guard and fired with them. Running besides, I outflanked them & took them in.

Three splendid horses & equipments were the result. I obtained a splendid bridle & breast strap by the operation. Following on, we picked up a number of stragglers. By night I had a bridle, pair of spurs, blanket, canteen, pocket knife & several other things. The blanket & knife I gave Willie. The trip paid me very well.

After remaining at Samaria Church during the middle of the day [June 14] & [the Legion] fell back while I voluntarily remained on picket to watch for some of our men who were beyond. I supposed the other works were guarded and to my astonishment [the] Division came running back [which told] me we were cut off & pursued by about 300 Cavalry.

We took to the woods & didn't have time to withdraw my pickets. We traveled thro' the timber at a lively rate and rode up to one of our outposts at 8 o'clock [P.M.], where the pickets took us to be Yanks & we thought them the same. Just as we were on the point of charging, supposing it to be the only means of escape, we found out they were rebels. We were then safe.

I remained at this latter post, [then I] hurry where to post sentinels & [I] left in time to escape being driven in as those fellows were at [Post] 1. I remained at one of the outposts and soon after daylight [June 15] the Yanks attacked again.[24]

[Brigadier General John R.] Cooke's N.C. troops marched out & fought them.[25] At this Co. H [Hampton Legion] rode in [to]

---

23   This is the action at Samaria Church.

24   Federal forces referred to this as a skirmish near Malvern Hill.

25   Cooke commanded the 15th, 27th, 46th, 48th, and 55th North Carolina regiments. This is the skirmish at Nance's Shop.

repulse them, opposing [them] with the scouts as there was more excitement about it. Taking the Chas. Cty. Road we found the enemy [line obliterated by a fold in the page]. ...while the regiment was engaged on the Malvern Hill road, but only slightly. After Cooke's brigade drove them off we were sent [to] the front to chase them. We deployed as skirmishers and charged them with [Captain L. F.] Smith's men [of the 10th Georgia Cavalry]. I rode in on horseback, was shot at by a sharpshooter but [was] not hit. We drove them off & followed — scout to the front. We soon found them & our company & Co. G were sent to charge again & did so, but learned the Yanks were too strong for our little command, tho we sent them flying to their reserves.

The next day, Thursday, [June 16] we went again to the front (scout) and saw the enemy entrench so [we had] no chance to pick them off. We then marched around the right & heard there were six pickets in the first house [word obliterated]. Three men dismounted, get in their rear, while seven of us were to charge anyone on horseback. The signal gun was fired and [word obliterated] we ducked, but the Yanks had discovered us & rode off to their skirmish line who opened fire on us fairly sharply. One bullet was sent thro the tail of [W. H.] Duva's horse & another took the skin from Duva's lower lip.[26] *No other casualty, but we missed the Yanks much to my regret.*

One hour after we rode to the front, and watched the Yanks, and when riding back across a field the enemy opened on us again. Flanking those shots we watched them carefully and fired on every one who showed himself. When going back the Yanks gave it to us again.

How I do like scouting, there is so much excitement and adventure but I decided to forfeit it to command my with the company.

Yesterday [Saturday, June 18] the enemy fell back, [we] dismissed those [for] we were invisible to them as always [two words obliterated] visited Charles City Co. Hse. Afterwards we went to Clarke's near the river and one of our batteries fired on the transports. In reply the gunboats shelled us. Killing one of the 24th

---

26 W. H. Duva served in Company H, Hampton Legion.
(Simpson, 1977, 450)

Va. [Cavalry]. With the week nearly passed and my life is still spared. Oh, how thankful I am for God's mercy & blessings. I think I shot several Yanks — I fired fifteen cartridges. At least four fellows shot at me. I felt a bullet go through my jacket sleeve — close shave. I am going to write Col. [Thomas] Logan for position as Adjutant of the Legion. Saw [Colonel Martin W.] Gary about becoming ordnance officer for the brigade. I may get it, but consider it doubtful. I want to get out of Co. H. Gary promised to do anything in his power for me, intervening to get [me] approved as an officer to command the scouts.

I have been on five scouts, three this week, & am still unhurt. God grant I may come out of every [one] of them as successfully. I feel that no one can cast a slur of any kind upon me for being absent at Dandrige [Tennessee].²⁷ I have vindicated myself in my own estimation & that of the Leg. If Major [Robert] Arnold (Col. Logan was wounded severely but is getting better) needs a good man he sends for Lt. Welch.²⁸ Such is my reputation with our regimental headquarters & with Gary, "Lt. Welch is a brave fellow."

I hope always to prove worthy of the name & strive to reflect deservedly upon my dear family & friends. I don't feel brave in what I regard to be courage, but God grant I may always act as a true officer should.

I saw Willie this morning; he is well & said he was going to write Sammie today. My horse is well but very tired. All the Yanks have left their side of the James River so we expect a few days rest and to be quiet.

I am quite well & in good spirits. I haven't received a letter from home since June 1st and Willie has allowed me to read all of his letters — 4 in number — & not one has come for me.

Well I reckon there are some on the way for me. Gives kisses and love to all for me. Love to Father, Sammie, Carrie & Maggie. Regards to all friends in Timmonsville. I wrote a long letter to Annie last Saturday, but before I could send it off we left.

---

27 See (Longstreet 1992, 533) for the explanation of the engagement near Dandridge.

28 Twenty-three year old Thomas Logan was wounded at Riddle's Shop on June 13, 1864. Thirty-one year old Robert Bolling Arnold became the acting lieutenant colonel of the Hampton Legion on May 19, 1864.
Robert K. Krick, *Lee's Colonels* (Dayton: Morningside Press, 1979, 33)

God grant that we may all come back safely. God bless & protect you all is my prayer. Kiss Robbie & Mary for me.

Yours most affectionately
Elliott

Excuse errors, etc.

Near the Drill House, Henrico Co.
[Monday] June 27th 1864

My dear Mother,

After two weeks of mental anxiety to say nothing of physical suffering, we are enjoying a day of rest. I have lately written you and Annie two letters each — something of five pages of foolscap each, so unless you have failed to get them I'll not bother you with the contents of either again.

Last Tuesday [June 21] as we were about going on another expedition, I concluded 'twould be best to go with the wagons as riding with several boils was quite unpleasant. Two days travel in the dust almost stifled and completely disgusted me, so going to Laurel Hill Church I domiciled with [Commissary Sergeant Donald J.] Auld & wrote, I think, Annie, but [I] am sure to Father.

Friday [June 24] being well enough to rejoin the regiment I started back and took my place Saturday [June 25] morning, having learned on my arrival of a pretty heavy fight the day before, but which knowing nothing about, I shall [leave it] to Willie to describe, he being in reserve & under fire.[29] [Major General Wade] Hampton says [Brigadier General Martin W.] Gary has a splendid brigade and good fighters.[30] The Legion & 24th Va. of our command were principally engaged.

As there seemed to be nothing doing in the front on Saturday [June 25] I decided to go beyond the pickets & find out what was going on; taking four of the Rutledges' [Company G, 7th South Carolina Cavalry], Willie among them, I rode toward Charles City C.H. where I found a strong picket. Learned Sheridan had crossed

---

29 Willie's letter did not survive the war. There was an action at Samaria Church and St. Mary's Church.

30 Gary received the promotion to brigadier general after the fight at Riddle's Shop. (Evans, 1987, 395-396)

his wagon train & most of his force at Wilcox's, and on meeting with a party of Va. scouts accompanied them around the Yanks, but finding out they didn't intend fighting, I came away, our horses being very much jaded. On the trip we found a Sergt. Taylor, from that County, who went with us & acted as guide. By his aid we were enabled to scour all around the enemy without them knowing of our proximity. We went to his house and his mother, a widow lady, gave us a luncheon, which was very acceptable indeed.[31] Toward evening, we stopt at Mrs. Clarke's and then returned to camp, just in time to hear the call to move off. It was 10 or 11 P.M. so we lay down and went to sleep.

Yesterday [June 26] we joined the command at Gatewoods as it started for this point and are now writing orders or something, but there being no Yankees in any force on the Peninsula now I hope our jaded animals & wearied men will have a little respite. Willie's squadron went on picket this morning, from which point (Chaffin's Bluff) he will probably write you.

The Yanks who were at Deep Bottom have left the picket force under cover of their gunboats and [have] withdrawn a force of 5,000 negroes & whites at Canneris — 20 miles below with the pickets in the river are all in our vicinity — & I hope none will come near.

Gary last night rec'd official notification of his promotion, so direct [the mail] in [the] future to "Gary's Brigade." [Captain John D.] Palmer is in Richmond, [acting Captain William G.] Gardner by some pretence has thrown the command of the company off on me & I in return have selected a spot for my "hdqrs." distant one or two hundred yards from the company, being fearful of contamination. Co (H) is consequently in high dudgeon at such treatment, but I have lost all interest in the worthless "Hoosiers," having but few friends left in it I am perfectly indifferent to its good or bad opinion. Maj. Arnold & Gen. Gary recognise me as nominally in command of the scouts & I have their permission to go out when I please, so such pettifoggers as Palmer & Gardner will not influence [me] one way or the other.

Two weeks ago today poor Smythe & Whitney were killed & now I learned my brother & bosom friend [George B.] Gelling

---

31   Without more information I could not identify this Mrs. Taylor.

has been sacrificed. When will this useless, terrible shedding of blood cease? To think poor Geo. is no more & think when we parted on James Island it was our last, I can't realise it & yet fear it is but too true. Oh, how sad, how solemn a warning & what a loss! No nobler man than Gelling ever lived. Activated by all the generous impulses that influence any one, he has passed from a sphere of usefulness to, I hope, a happy eternity. God grant it may be so, & tho' parted here, I trust we may meet above. Palmer's brother too I hear has been killed, & [U.S.] Grant has notified his men that fighting has ceased & with the pick & spade the siege has begun. In all his artifices and devilish devices he has been heretofore failed — the same Power rules & will direct our Chieftains. On Him alone we must rely & patiently await the issue.

Your most welcome letter of the 15th was rec'd several days ago & sensibly relieved me for I feared I had been <u>neglected</u> but not forgotten; it was the first from you since the 30th of May & none but a few papers have come from Annie since the 1st inst.

[Major General Augustus] Kautz, that Yankee Dutchman, has again severed our railroad but I hope, & in fact have heard, they are again running the train; if so we shall get our mails regularly again. Willie says his papers haven't come, is inclined to think someone else reads them.

[Lieutenant General Wade] Hampton, I think, has gone on the Southside [Railroad] with his cavalry & I hope will do as good work there as they have done this side of [the James] — he has a splendid command. We are situated in the neighborhood of the river and can get a beautiful view of it & the gunboats at the risk of a "lamp-post".[32] Just now I heard a few of those hugh missles exploding near by & suppose the cause to be the curiosity of a few visitors. The men are accustomed to such things, but the horses get somewhat alarmed at the loud reports.

Capt. [Josiah K.] McNeely [Company D] & [Second] Lt. [James R.] Huff [Company E] of our regt. [were] wounded lately [and] have both died — they were good officers & brave men.[33]

---

32 Army slang for the heavy projectile fired by a gunboat's ordnance.

33 McNeely and probably Huff, were mortally wounded on June 13, 1864 at Riddell's Shop. The captain, died on June 17 and the lieutenant on an unspecified time during that month. Both enlisted as privates in 1861.
(Simpson, 1977, 423, 430)

Willie has rec'd his tin case & paper; having a good supply in Richmond I will not call upon him yet awhile. If you can send me ten or fifteen dollars I should be nicely obliged. I haven't a cent and don't know when we shall draw. Before I expected to have been paid off, or should have written sooner for it.

It is beginning to cloud up & look like rain. Oh what a long, dry, hot spell we have had! Oftentimes when guide near the enemy we would take them for our own men — their blue coats being entirely gray with dust. I never knew a worse time anywhere.

We are going to have rice and peas for dinner today — regular ration. Applications have been made from Hd Qrs for flour for variety's sake, if nothing else. June apples keep us from scurvy, but vegetables are delicacies & great scarcities. A little rain would give us [illegible] corn three or four weeks, and as soon as the ears fill I hope to see every Yankee driven from our shore.

We remember how the assyrians were treated, God [page missing]

Bivouac near Malvern Hill, Va.
[Sunday] July 3rd 1864

Well Dear Mother & Annie

I've written you repeatedly but suppose as in Tenn. our communications are cut off tho' I hope they will speedily be resumed. Having but a few moments to write I cannot enter into details. Should the mails ever reach you there will be two letters for each of you, of about 5 pages of foolscap in each communication.

Knowing it to [be] customary for such things I wrote to Col. [Thomas] Logan to ask what chance I stood for the Adjutancy of the Legion & tho' I failed to procure it, Yet the tenor of the Col.'s reply was such as to make me feel quite proud. He is a man of few words, consistent & sincere. I enclose it for you both to read & for Annie to put away among my treasures. Like all smart men, he writes [with] a poor hand & [it] may puzzle you to read it.

Yesterday [July 2] I went to Richmond to get some things from my trunk. Found tho' only tied, it was quite safe = nothing had been touched. Richmond is remarkably dull and dreadful hot. Not having any extra funds I could [not] get dinner & found it advisable to return to camp.

Having had a gun, or pistol pointed at me on several occasions by some of our men I procured a pair of nice gray pantaloons & a pair of fine English shoes, so am well fitted as for clothing. While out scouting a pair of blue trousers with one of our dark gray jackets is apt to make a man think a Yank was in front of him.

Willie is still on picket at Chaffin's Bluff, where his squadron is enjoying itself hugely. He was quite well yesterday, tho' I haven't seen him for a week.

Since the roads were cut we have drawn no corn for our horses. Oats & clover constitute our horse's feed. Fortunately we have had no work lately & our animals get on tolerably well. I can fire my pistol from mine now, tho' he is still very scared at the report of a gun.

Still no rain, but oceans of dust and a scorching sun which almost boils. [Captain John D.] Palmer & [1st Lieutenant William G.] Gardner are here. P. is complaining but in camp. I have at last with Frank [P.] Hughes help succeeded in "flanking" Co. H in the [1st Sergeant E. J.] Dumaresa question: Logan told me yesterday he was going to have him appointed Lieut. in the co. & for him to say so is equivalent to its consummation. How the Co. will storm but it is due to D. & I shall not care. To get out now myself is my main consideration.

Do write & let me know if the report be true about Geo. Gelling's death. I've thought much of it & can't convince myself of its truth. Oh, how sad & tho' great is my loss yet how serious a loss to his relatives & friends. Hughes & I shall [write] an obituary notice & send it to the "Courier" if it be true. Whitney, Smythe & Gelling — three intimate friends gone in so short a time — what a solemn warning. "Oh, God prepare me for the final change" is my daily prayer & hourly wish.

Tomorrow [July 4] will be the anniversary of the fall of Vicksburg, but Richmond is still under the Keeping of a Higher power, guarded by men who never knew defeat.

The stupendous efforts put forth by our enemies must surely exhaust their strength very soon. Crowds of deserters arrive daily who have never even been to their regiments, and represent Grant's men as whipped & badly.

Some move is afloat. So great silence on both sides augurs something sharp & that very shortly. Our Father in Heaven will surely turn it in our favor.

I have written in so great haste I fear you will not be able to read [it], but take it well for the deed.

Give much love to Father, Carrie, Sammie, Maggie. Kiss the little ones for me, God bless you, dear ones, and spare our lives for a reunion on earth to pray to & praise Him is my daily prayer.

Yours most affectionately
Elliott

Legion Camp, Darbytown Road
[Monday] July 18th 1864

Dear Mother,

Saturday's mail brought me a second letter from Annie, the first being the date of June 22nd & the last July 9th both of which were very acceptable, but dreadfully short. I saw yours to Willie of date and look for one myself today.

Last week I was greatly debilitated by a pretty severe [attack] of diarrhoea and was weakened but am now quite well. The very hot oppressive weather & irregular diet doubtless produced it. Two delightful showers last week cooled the atmosphere delightfully & we now have nights that require two blankets & occasionally fires and days with pleasant breezes tho the sun at midday is disagreeably hot.

Yesterday was Sunday [July 17] & I intended writing you but the Quartermaster came up to pay off the men & being the only officer in the company who could make out the payroll I had to go over, get the money & pay the men. [Captain John D.] Palmer might have done the paying off but neither he nor [1st Lieutenant William G.] Gardner could make out a roll. G. ought to be court martialed for grounds — he absolutely knows nothing & holds the position of 1st Lieut. in the CSA. Think of him in England as a representative of our Army. I am not jealous, but ashamed that the Co., & myself should have such a character in it. After paying off [the men] there was but little time left so I postponed writing till this morning.

Last Saturday [July 16] our company was detailed to go as wagon guard to the neighborhood of Chas. Cty. C.H. for oats, while

the regt. went to Tilghman's gate as support for a battery of artillery intended to shell a pontoon bridge & some gunboats. Our
service was decidedly preferable. The demoralizing effect of a "Pa.
Dutch oven," [word illegible] also is too great, so I went on my
way rejoicing, knowing my horse would be benefitted by the trip.
The Legion went down & soon after opening this huge shell came
howling over their heads. What injury was inflicted, I've been
unable to learn, but I know that the H. Leg. was shelled out of
camp, tho' nobody was hurt.

Our company went down to Wilcox's farm and while they
were gathering forage I went out to Mr. Clarke's to see them. Mrs.
Clarke & the young ladies came out & shook hands with me. We
had a pleasant chat for some time with news of the day. Being
near the Yankee lines they seldom see any papers and I took several
of the late ones down to them. At noon I was in the point of starting, but they all insisted on my remaining to dinner. As there was
a prospect of getting some vegetables I remained & wasn't disappointed either. Corn bread & bacon had become so tiresome that
I couldn't resist the prospect of a change. I left about 4 o'clock after
a charming visit. The young ladies were very agreeable & I had
to play the gallant which I can first do & no mistake. The youngest
daughter Miss Laura is a capital girl.[34] [I] will have to call again,
as I rec'd a very cordial invitation to do so.

I wish everything was quiet so we could go down there &
encamp in the neighborhood. There are some charming people
living on those plantations. Don't be surprised if I take one some
of these days & a young lady to boot, or simply in an attachment.

Some time ago I wrote Col. Logan asking if he had not yet
appointed his Adjutant for the position. My note was so worded
that it could not be regarded as undignified or ungentlemanly in
my making the request, nor would it lower me in the Col.'s estimation. His reply was neat & to the point, informing me that his selec-

---

34   There were as many people named Wilcox as Taylor on the Peninsula. Without more
information, they could not be tracked down.
      The only Clarke family in Charles City County with a daughter named Laura was John J.
Clarke (age 50) and his wife Margaret J. (age 51). They had five children: Amanda M. (age 23),
Mary J. (age 21), Virginia E. (age 20), Trent A. (age 17), Laura (age 17), and Octavia (age 14).
      Entry for John J. Clarke, Charles City County, VA, Census of the Population, (NA Microfilm,
roll 1340, 179), Records of the Census, 1860, NA, Virginia.

tion was with [Frank P.] Hughes, a former member of his company & an intimate friend I know. I sent his note home in a letter to you to read & save for me.

Palmer confidentially informed me recently of his having made application for [1st Sergeant E. J.] Dumaresa's appointment as Lieut. in the company. I didn't confer the same honor upon or bestow the same confidence in him & tell him I had been working for the identical thing [for] six months. It is a necessity & not from choice that he has taken action in the matter, for Col. Logan sent him word he didn't intend the company should have an election.

The Capt. [John D. Palmer] I believe in very many things is a well disposed man, but he's absentminded, vacillatory, and quick tempered, & I am willing to make all allowances for him. But for Gardner no matter how much I may desire to admit for him, the daily manifestations of his detestable manners are so palpable that it is utterly impossible to be charitable toward him. I can forgive him and his act but to forget it [it] is necessary that memory should perish or reason forsake me. To have him Capt. of the Co. would be a sufficient excuse to tender a resignation.

Major [Robert B.] Arnold, or Old Granny, as we call him, is still in command. Arnold is a brave man and clever fellow, but the slightest case I know of; — he assumes no responsibility, is afraid of [Lieutenant Beaufort W.] Ball (Gary's Adjutant) and many of the foolish things he is guilty of, besides which I can go to him & talk him into anything I wish.[35] I am glad to know Logan will back in a couple of weeks, then may we back out of a revision of everything.

Everything is remarkably quiet; there are no Yanks on our side of the [James] river. Grant continues to send troops and transports down the river, while the report of a gun from his side of the river is rarely heard.

Prices still are going up in Richmond till beyond all reason. It is a fortunate thing that Congress allowed officers one ration each at the end of the month. The gold lace men would be indebted to the Government. Government prices are as follows: Bacon 50¢ [per pound], flour 70¢, rice $1.00, peas 50¢, Sugar $20.00, cof-

---

35   Roster of the Hampton Legion, (NA Microfilm, roll 362), NA.

STEPHEN ELLIOTT WELCH OF THE HAMPTON LEGION

fee $10.00 put thro' an increase since the fore part of last week of an 100% on most of the articles. Couldn't afford to keep a servant on those prices, so Frank [P. Hughes] & I mess with [Commissary Sergeant] Donald [Auld] who has [a servant] & can feed a boy.

Tell Annie I should like to see that country friend that was with her bound if she is <u>very</u> pretty and [the] inducement will have to be very great for me to put myself out of the way to see them.

I have heard but once from Petersburg since coming from Tennessee to which I sent two answers. Miss W. had attempted the sarcastic in her communications but my first reply proved I think I was more than her match tho' and fearing I had offended her by being too sharp in some matters, wrote a second in a milder tone, but to neither have I rec'd a reply & don't expect one.

Addie & Auld correspond, but tho' he has sent six [letters] no reply has reached him yet. As an Irishman would say. "Barrin' all ye good people" I don't know of a woman on earth that I'd write to six times if my communications remained unanswered — if in fact I felt sure of one's being unanswered, it would be my last, by the time three went unless I'd the best of reasons for thinking my letters lost the matter would trouble me no more. Think of six? How devoted — not any for me in that style.

I asked Annie if you had not sent any funds to me to return them as I had drawn pay to first of April but should the money come I'll let Willie have it. The "V." [five dollar bill] was used, many thanks. I shall keep my letter open till the mail comes & then add a "P.S." if there is anything for me.

We have no papers, yet this morning, but report says Early is recrossing the Potomac, retreating and if he conducts his retrograde as successfully as his advance movement I shall regard him worthy of promotion. He has kept Yankeedom in a fever of excitement and Gov. [Andrew] Curtin of Pa. couldn't get his gallant Pa. Dutch "Milish" to turn out in sufficient numbers for him — good sign.[36] I guess they think there have been enough men killed in the war and that one hundred days troops should [have] a slim chance of getting badly hurt once in the field.

---

36   "Milish" means militia.

I wrote some pretty long letters during the succession of mail communications which I hope you and Annie have rec'd as this. They contained detailed accounts of our fights. Willie also wrote you both what his regt had been doing. Should nothing happen I want to go down to see him this evening and spend one hour or live down at the Hill.

We are both thank God enjoying excellent health and are in good spirits. Much love to Father, Sammie, Carrie & Maggie. Give my love to & kiss Annie, Robbie & Mary for me. Accept love from both of us, & my constant prayers are that if God see fit he may reunite [us]. God bless you all.

Your affectionate Son
Elliott

Near Rowland's Mill, Chas. City Co. Va.
[Thursday] August 11th 1864

Dear Mother,

After a long lapse of time the effect of which was to make me think all were going to stop writing. I rec'd a long letter from Annie of the 24th ult. I was satisfied with it and accept it in lieu of half a dozen shorter ones. Tell Annie I'll answer it pretty soon, if an opportunity from scouting is allowed now.

The day after I wrote Annie last [Wednesday, August 3], I went down to Mr. Clarke's to spend part of the day with them in company with a Mr. Harrid. We spent a delightful morning and just after dinner one of the men came up & told me Gen. Gary sent an order to me to get out of my position as best I could, that we were cut off. The family was in a state of alarm, partly at the thought of several rebels being captured & the prospect of having another Yank force around them.

We started and travelled 20 miles before coming upon a Yankee & wouldn't have seen him but for turning out of our course. After passing Riddle's Shop we fully expected to find the regiment in the Chas. City road, but two miles were passed without seeing a soul so we took a cross road connecting with the New Market route ran afoul of their picket line.[37] *A Dutchman stopped us by*

---

37 The Federals called this the action near Wilcox's Landing.

saying, "Holt! Holt, dare! Vere you go dare?" [W. H.] Duva told him he was just going to his friends, when he mounted & we left instantly.

That was about 10 P.M. Soon after we saw a dark object going across a field & I told Duva to follow it, which he did for a while, but as it moved off he couldn't follow; we heard enough ten minutes afterward to satisfy us in not pursuing as it was a squadron of Yankee Cavalry returning after finding our pickets & firing on them.

Our Dutch friend shot into the bushes where we had been about 5 minutes after leaving, having first called the "Sajent" to know if "I mus' shoot?" If there hadn't been so many of them he would have had a chance of firing.

On reaching our brigade, we had to stand in a pool of water for ten minutes before the 24th Va. [Cavalry] could be satisfied that we were rebels and came near firing into us.

The next morning [Thursday, August 4] I rode near the head of the Infantry column — Kershaw's brigade — and it commenced firing, branching to the left I took a small road leading to the Chas. City [Road] (having soon after daylight gone to the Darbytown Road with six of the scouts) to go to the Legion, hearing it was engaged in a skirmish. Riding carelessly along, I thought we should strike the road in rear of our breastworks, but came out 400 yards in front and directly in sight, upon which the 7th [South Carolina] Reg't. opened on us.

I was standing sideways to the works & can't imagine how neither horse nor rider was grazed. Not one in the party was touched, neither party was to blame, for but a short time before we rode out, some Yankee cavalry rode up to survey our batteries & were driven off; we came in sight & Duva having on blue trousers & another man a blue coat, they took us to be Yanks & fired. Nothing of any consequence happened during the balance of the day & matters looking quiet on Friday [August 5] I went to the rear to have my horse shod.

Saturday afternoon [August 6] the enemy had disappeared & I started for the Co. Ho. to find out by what route they had retreated. As they came, they retired across the pontoons at Deep Bottom. Willie can give you an idea of their advance, having been *in the fight. Riding back toward the river on Sunday morning [August 7], our friends were very glad to see us & know the enemy had disappeared.*

The Misses Clarke wanted me to stay all day, but it could not be did you know. I went to the river bank & saw the steamers pass & concluded to report at once in order to get my "scouts" back again.

Monday [August 8], we reoccupied "our line" and Tuesday night [August 9] such was the nature of my report that Gen. Richard Ewell ordered a battery of artillery down to fire at their transports which are daily passing down laden with men & horses, & now we were to open on them.

Tuesday night I heard a report of the landing of some Yankee artillery at Haxhall's from which point my communications could be cut off, so taking a man with me I went down yesterday morning [August 10] & found the report false. At that time I was unaware the Legion was in the neighborhood, but there it was in the road awaiting orders & artillery. I started for Wilcox's Landing knowing that to be the best point to fire from & Gen. [Martin W.] Gary sent for me, introduced me to Col. [T. H.] Carter, commanding the artillery, who asked my opinion about the boats, positions on the river, etc. & then we all went down to Swinard's Bluff and waited for the Yanks.[38]

The mail steamer "J. Brooks" came first with negro soldiers, but unfortunately the guns weren't in position, so she slipped by. The str. "Connecticut" went down empty; she wasn't worth wasting ammunition on. An ocean steamer with cavalry aboard drove by, but our fuzes were behind. A tug with boxes & stalls apparently, and another tug with three schooners & two flats all moving very slowly. They came abreast the battery & bang went a bolt.

It was grand. I stood alongside the guns & enjoyed the sport hugely. For one hour we had it our way, then came a gunboat & at long last shot over & under us. The seven boats were all struck, more or less & I think one of the steamers disabled.

The gunboat, a wooden thing, stood in dread of us apparently, & wouldn't come too close till the battery left, then becoming

---

38   Carter served as Jubal Early's chief of artillery.

as bold as a lion the craft came close in shore & alarmed the poor citizens by exploding shells at their doors.

I sat in Mr. Clarke's piazza and the huge missiles burst all around the house, but principally in the field just in front of the door. I took matters as cooly as tho' I didn't mind them a bit, consequently the ladies, didn't put themselves out of the way, for safe keeping at all. Once I advised them to go in the cellar, but two objected & I said nothing more.

They gave me some nice ripe damsons, greengages, peaches & pears, all of which Bro. Steve enjoyed exceedingly.[39] *One of the young ladies gave me some geranium leaves & pansies. When no Yankees are about, scouting is very pleasant pastime for we can occasionally drop in and see a friend, but these Virginia girls, what can I say for them — they're almost sure to turn a youth's mind, but they can't cause that in me now, bein' as how I'se cut my eye tooth.*

Willie is very well; decidedly fat & dirty — has quite a reputation in his company & "if he keeps on, as he's begun" why he will soon be covered with "<u>mud & glory</u>." as Col. [Napoleon Bonaparte] Bratton said of [Brigadier General Micah] Jenkin's [South Carolina] brigade last winter. He gave me a long letter to read, from Sammie. While I'm writing the gunboats & our lads are at it & but for writing you I should have been down there. Today the firing is from Berkeley, the birthplace of W. H. Harrison, Ex. Pres. [of the] U.S.

I wanted to send a paper to Miss Bradley out as our battery came away. I suppose the Yanks have sent a land force to the point, so I can't get there, but some time today I'll scout round there & see what's the prospect. A newspaper is the most acceptable thing these isolated people & we get, and I believe it is the reason I always find a pleasant time at Mr. Clarke's for at every opportunity I send them the latest news.

When we left this country last Wednesday [August 3] we just got out in time for the next day, "a whole power o' men" came down to hunt us up; they were gallant enough to steal everything from a poor woman living in the woods & therafter to burn her

---

39   I could not identify Steve.

house for "aiding" & "Abetting the rebellion." The cowardly villains stole $250 from Mrs. Rowland & were going to burn her mill, but she saved it & had her money restored. While rummaging for rebels, they carried off anything of value & only trusted themselves, tho' 150 in number after 13 men, a mile or two from their gunboat.

There's a spy near our camp & I only want to find him out. Monday two of my scouts took a Yank and got $200 in green-backs from him. Some prisoners were taken yesterday by the wagon guard and allowed to go "scott free," one had five lbs. of coffee & sugar. Well, I'll look out for the next lot.

I am enjoying most excellent health and Spirits. At last accounts our box hadn't arrived but we look for it daily, hope it will come shortly. I am very sorry to hear you were all so ill and am very thankful you have recovered.

Kiss Annie, Robbie, Harry & Carrie for me. Yesterday was Carrie's birthday. God grant she may live to see many more. Much love to Father, Sammie & all enquiring friends. Regards to Mrs. Keith & family & all acquaintances. God bless you dear Mother and all of our loved ones, and spare us to be reunited is my daily prayer.

> *Your affectionate Son*
> *Elliott*

> *In the trenches, Deep Bottom*
> *[Tuesday] August 30th 1864*

My dear Mother.

Your very welcome letter of the 24th was rec'd a while ago. I was happy to hear from you & to know that you are all well. Sorry you haven't rec'd the money I sent you. It must have been stolen by some one. There was $80 — in the Old Issue in it. Did you receive the Yankee papers & letters & likenesses I sent you? I wrote you a letter giving you an account of our fighting & c. last week. Hope you rec'd it. I wrote Carrie & Sammie a few days ago.

The package I rec'd on Friday last, & it so happened that Ellie had first called to see me, having been to see Gen. Gary on business. I opened it, & found it filled, and as all things from home always are, with articles [which are] particularly acceptable. The cake was very nice, & the pickles also. I gave Ellie the coffee & sugar mark-ed for him & also the pickles as he is fond of them. He didn't take the rice but left it with me. The shirt is a very pretty, nice fitting one, & has been much admired by our men. I cannot thank you too much for all the nice things contained in the package. The hand-kerchiefs were quite acceptable, & the coffee, & sugar were a great treat. The papers altho' old, contained considerable news to me. The bundle had been in Richmond almost two weeks, but I had no way of getting it, as the enemy were on this side [of the river]. Ellie told me to thank you very much for his share of the contents.

He was looking well healthy & sported a nice black felt hat, & [a] pair of shoes he got from the Yankees. I've got a nice pair of grey pants [which] I drew last week, but they are too long for me.

I'm glad to hear that Pa is so much better. I knew he'd im-prove under you & sister Annie's kind treatment. He was fortunate in being at home when you had such an abundance of good things. It affords me considerable pleasure to know that your corn, peas, & vegetables have got along so well.

I regret to hear that Harrie doesn't like his studies; he ought to devote his attention to them at his age, for if he doesn't he'll be sorry for it in after life. Tell Robbie to persevere in his studies & he'll become a smart man.

Yesterday Don Auld invited me over to dine with him, & I went, & had a delightful dinner. It consisted of tomatoes stew, squashes, cucumbers, beef-steak fried with onions, cornbread, & watermelon to wind up with. I enjoyed it very much, I assure you. Beef has been issued to us several times lately, but having no way to cook it — I prefer it to bacon.

Our Reg't is now on the New Market Road. Today our Co. [G] on the skirmish line, but everything is quiet. Last night I saw Joe Clarke [Company E, 1st Texas], brother of the former Lieut. [T. A. G. Clarke] in Ellie's Co. He is now in the 1st Texas Reg.'t., & looks like a different man.[40]

I have got so [that] if it rains at night I have a blanket to cover me. I consider myself well-off — a person of circumstances.

---

40   Joseph A. Clark transferred from Company A, Hampton's Legion to the 1st Texas in July 1862. He spent most of 1863 in the hospital and received his parole from the Federal government on April 12, 1865 at Appomattox Court House, Virginia.
(Simpson, 1977, 40)

I am truly very thankful to our Heavenly Father for merciful-ly preserving my life & health during this campaign. I now feel my dependence on Him who alone can save & hope that I shall ere long be a true Christian. If only I had a friend here to Explain & simplify the great truths contained in the Scriptures. It would be a great consolation to me. I pray that God may change my heart & that my Eyes may be opened to the glorious light of the Gospel. I feel now a great desire to become a good & holy man, & trust that my thoughts may not be diverted from this subject by gay & thoughtless companions. Pray for me, dear Mother, that I may speedily be converted & become a good & upright man.

I became acquainted with a lady who has a family of seven, the Eldest of whom is now 16 years, & the next one [is] a little suffered from pleurisy, & she is in rather destitute circumstances; they are a very nice family, & seem to think so much of each other. I have given out my washing to them several times, & the lady is now making me a vest out of the Yankee overcoat I captured. I wish it was in my power to assist them, altho' the neighbors are very kind & furnish them [with] the necessities of life. I was there last week, & they gave me some very nice new cider, & as many apples as I could Eat & made me stay to dinner. Ellie knows them, & they esteem him very highly.

I was speaking with some of the Legion some time ago & was told that Ellie was very highly thought of by his Company, & Reg't., & they would like to see him [made] Capt. He is highly thought of by Col. Logan & Gen. Gary.

Well, I must close. Love to all the dear ones at home, & kind regards to all friends.

Write soon, God bless & protect you always is my earnest prayer.

Your affectionate Son
Willie

Upshore, Chas. City County, Va.
[Wednesday] Aug. 31st 1864

Dear Mother,

Yours of the 25th came last night. I hope ere this you've heard from me. I wrote before we were cut off but could not send my letters away to tell [why] the communications were fewer.

Last Friday [August 26] I rode up to camp to see Gary, Logan & Haskell and make some arrangements for remaining down here, procuring home feed etc.

I am now in command of this Dept. with twelve select men & as much liberty [and] as wide a command (tho' not so many men) as a Brig. In fact I wouldn't swap with some of them. My orders are to arrest any treacherous citizens, watch movement on the river, as well as the force toward Cumming's, capture all Yankees & confiscate their possession[s] except deserters & go generally as I please.

Last Sunday [August 28] before daylight two of my party were watching a road, & caught 10 Jews, who were trying to escape to the Yankees. They had a large amount of gold & silver coin, greenbacks, & two watches which we confiscated & sent the prisoners to Richmond. In the division of [the] spoils my share was $27 in gold, $22 in Greenbacks & $13 in State bills. Enclosed I send a dollar each for Carrie, Robbie & Harry. The balance I shall exchange for Confederate money.

Monday [August 29] morning I rode down the County in hope of capturing some Yanks who were in the habit of coming out for fruit & vegetables as well as for information generally, but tho' I learned some of the events that daily transpire I couldn't catch any of the fellows.

I shall go down again tonight for some remaining negroes and try a scheme for "bagging" a few of the "blue jackets" the only ones from whom any information reliable can be obtained without acting as spy & go inside their lines.

Old Judge Gregory, living below us, is as clever a man as I've seen.[41] *The Yankees have threatened all who live there with the total destruction of their property if they feed any of the scouts. Notwithstanding this, the Judge invited us in, gave us a capital supper and plenty for our horse[s] to eat for which he wouldn't dream of accepting a cent.*

I saw Willie when I went to camp recently, he was quite well & I hope God will spare his life. I am quite well & in good spirits for which I am truly thankful.

---

41   I could not identify Judge Gregory.

Give my love to Annie, Carrie, Harry, & Robbie. Kiss them for me. Love to Father and Sammie. Regards to Mrs. Keith, & family, Mrs. Wells (and all inquiring friends.)

Weather is pleasant and everything around us is happily arrayed.

Tell Annie I shall write her in a few days.

> *God bless you is my daily prayer.*
> *Your affectionate Son*
> *Elliott*

Chapter Three

Operations Along the
Chickahominy River (1864)

Near Chas. City C.H.
[Thursday] September 8th 1864

Dear Mother,

No letter this week from home for me makes me think the mails are to blame or home folks are sick but should nothing happen I shall look for one by this or tomorrow's mail.

Well nothing more has happened of consequence on my "line" since writing last, which I did to Annie, a few days ago and enclosed $50 for Harry & Carrie. A letter written prior to that to yourself contained three gold dollars, both of which I hope have reached you ere this. I mention these matters, as Willie sent me his last from home stating the money he sent had not been rec'd.

One day this week I rode to within one or two hundred yards of the enemy lines at Berkeley in hopes of drawing a few of them after me into an ambuscade, but they have told the neighbors they daily intend[ed] firing on us, [and] except they capture us it isn't their intention to molest the party. How considerate! Should any of them come out, I shall not have so much regard for their precious bodies.

A great deal of travelling daily takes place on the river; troops pass up & down, army wagons, ambulances & artillery go both ways and wherever the enemy is to be found, he reports his intention of remaining all winter. If Grant remains, I hope the James will freeze & then for "horse marines" to which [General Joseph] Wheeler's would be but a circumstance.

Monday [September 5] evening last I rode across the County to the vicinity of Forge Bridge & Bradley's Ford, in the Chicka-

54

hominy. After attending to some business, my comrade & I called on some very nice families & made the acquaintance of some charming young ladies, among whom were the Misses Lou & Lucy Christian. These ladies gave us some music & insisted on my helping to sing. Of course I did my prettiest.

The young lady from Richmond I wrote Annie about has returned to her home. Her parents heard of the Yankees landing at Berkeley & sent for her. If some of these girls knew how <u>deep</u> an impression they made on my mind they'd cut my acquaintance. Lucky thing people don't think aloud or there might be a terrible fuss raised in this world of <u>our'n</u>. Miss Atkinson was the name of the young lady alluded to above & a sillier specimen of humanity I never saw.[1] To sit, hands folded in her lap & talk of belle & beaux was her delight & only occupation that I know of.

On my return from Forge bridge a young man residing in the County, who wished to get his negroes away, came down with an order from Gary for me to render all assistance in my power. Taking six or eight men, we rode down yesterday & brought back nine very likely negroes who were making preparations for leaving, in fact, had been packed up several times to start. I had met the young man before. He seemed very much indebted for our help.

We rode down to within a mile of the Yankee's stronghold at Cannaris & in returning I brought back a horse & mule which Gen. [Gilman] Marston, commanding at C., had loaned a lot of runaway slaves.[2] I broke up a nest of these freshs to our community & told them if I ever found them there again I'd blow up everything in their presence. I guess those negroes will think me a "hard case," & I'll prove a terror to that portion of Charles City that continues its evil doing.

Gen. [Martin W.] Gary in recommending me to Mr. Christian remarked to him that I deserved promotion & had been rendering very efficient service to the country for the past two months. That appears as tho' I was in G.'s good graces & I hope always to prove ever the [recipient] of such an opinion. The "promotion" part is

---

1   I could not identify this individual.

2   Ezra J. Warner, *Generals in Blue* (Baton Rouge: Louisiana State University Press, 1964), 312.

Pleasant to think of for I may yet be put over Gardner — either made Captain of the Company if Palmer is placed on the "Retired list" or promoted to the rank of 1st Lieut. and permanently in command of the Scouts. If any choice were allowed me I'd take the latter for I have more liberty than any Captain in the brigade & wouldn't exchange places.

Frank Hughes has lost a brother — Toni — at Petersburg by capture. He was taken prisoner some days ago. I want a Yankee deserter to come along or else bag a prisoner to get some "Greenbacks" for poor Toni's benefit.

Have you heard that Willie Hughes was dead? He died on the 3rd of August & has gone to a happy home. I am truly sorry for poor Mrs. Hughes & deeply sympathize with her, but what a consolation to know her loss is her son's Eternal gain.[3]

I wonder what Mrs. Gregory has done with herself now that Atlanta has fallen.[4] I am very sorry for that poor family. They must be in very great distress. I am badly disappointed in the evacuation of Atlanta & tho' matters are bad enough they might indeed have been much worse.

Well, a Higher Power is guiding us & has our destiny in His keeping. What He sees fit for us I am willing to submit to & believe it for the best.

With one or two exceptions I have succeeded in making friends of all the inhabitants of this county. Deep in the woods, in a regular old Va. homestead, resides a family of Gentry, the mother of which is a good old lady & I feel myself perfectly at home whenever I go there. Should rations come out short then I can go there & get dinner, supper, or if early enough a breakfast without feeling that I am intruding.

Old Mrs. Gentry is very motherly indeed & I am half persuaded she has taken a fancy to me, at all events Mrs. Southall (a married daughter) tells me I can write home & tell my folks I've found another mother but then she can never be no matter how kind, such a mother as I have. God has blessed me wonderfully in raising me up friends wherever I go as much as in any other way.

---

3   Mrs. Hughes did not appear in the census of 1860.

4   I could not identify this individual.

Now dear Mother and Annie also, you must forgive me if my letters are not as long and frequent as when with the command, but depend in it I shall write you both at every opportunity, tho' it's needless to assure you of this. Duty, Gratitude would demand it of me if I failed to regard it a pleasure so be assured.

"I think of the absent and waft them

A Whispered 'Good Night'" at the loss of every day of my existence.

As the property of aliens and particularly of escaping foreigners is confiscated, I was allowed by Gen. Gary to keep the specie like which I took from the Israelites & divided among my party. My share of gold I disposed of at 20 for 1 and gave Willie $100. To Sammie I sent $50 & $25 for Carrie & Harry. Please accept the enclosed, as I know of nothing to give you & you can get something that will prove useful.

For Annie I have a beautiful little Colt's repeater for her & will send it home at the first opportunity. Excepting, I can share with my loved ones, I feel no pleasure in having anything.

My scouting trip has been very renumerative for after clearing myself of debt I shall have about $300 in pocket and the Government owes me $450 more.

The weather is quite like Autumn; the clouds which so long have been "high & dry" at last gave forth their gentle showers and besides refreshing us greatly have benefitted the late crops of the section greatly.

I have written to Willie's Col. [Alexander Cheves Haskell] & Capt. asking their permission to let him come down & spend a few days with me. I've also invited Frank Hughes to come & if they get off will come tomorrow.

I've become quite a friend of the family of Clarke, [which] I wrote you of and after talking of Willie & Frank so much they are quite anxious to see who & what my favorites are like. I hope to satisfy their curiosity. Speaking of the Clarkes, I don't know when I've seen three more interesting young ladies than those daughters. One of them intend writing to her brother. who is wounded & in Richmond to apply for a detail in my party. As he is a brave intelligent man I shall be pleased to have him.

Miss Lizzie Walker continues to do my picketing on the river, thereby relieving us of much arduous duty, attended with considerable danger.[5]

We are about making up a purse of $50 or $60 in Yankee money for her brother who is a prisoner at Point Lookout, to be given to the young lady & as she idolizes her brother I can conceive of nothing more acceptable.

I contemplate a visit in a few nights to our kind friend Mrs. Roland, who lives now under Yankee rule & about 100 yards from their pickets. Taking the dark hours to do so, I think it can be done with perfect safety — to say nothing of seeing her, [that] the information I would gain would recompense for any danger or trouble I may put myself to.

Are we to have Peace, or is their voice still for War? When such ultra peace men as Harris & Long will compromise with McClellan's party I think there's hope. God grant it and speedily may this dreadful question be settled.

Willie & I continue in excellent health for which I am truly grateful.

Much love to Father & Sammie. Heaps of love to Annie, Carrie, Harry & Robbie. Kiss them all for me. Accept much love, dearest Mother and I daily pray God to continue His blessings to our family. Remember me to Mrs. Keith & family and all enquiring friends.

> *Your loving Son*
> *Elliott*

Hd. Qrs. H. Legion
[Sunday] Oct. 9th '64

Dear Mother & Sisters,

Mournful indeed is my task, but I must perform it. Misfortunes never came singly & I have a number to recount. First I lost some of my clothing followed by my horse, bridle & saddle; next I learned of the death of poor [Second Sergeant] Willie [H.] Simmons [Company H].[6] *On Friday evening [October 7] I was told Willie was taken*

---

5 I could not find Miss Walker in the 1860 census.

6 Simmons was killed in action on September 29, 1864 at Chaffin's Farm. (Simpson, 1977, 449)

prisoner, next that Frank [P. Hughes] was mortally wounded, & yesterday [October 8] I went to see him & found Charlie [A.] Gregory, formerly of our company, a corpse, & now [Arthur] Harbin [Company C] is captured.[7]

Last Thursday [October 6] Col. [Thomas M.] Logan told me I could take a few men with me & try to capture a picket post, to get a horse. Going in [the] rear of the enemy I found it impractical to capture the men at White's Tavern & I sent word to Col. L. to send me 15 men & I'd try to take another much less strongly posted & turned down the [road] came to see the Clarkes, Walkers & others for whom I had some letters & papers.

Later at night I stopped on Mrs. W., a widow, she came out & we had a long talk with her. Harbin was with me. Early next morning [October 7] I saw the Clarkes, Wilcoxes, Christians & Wares but hearing very heavy firing on the north side we hurried up the Chas. City road.

On approaching White's Tavern [we] were told our men had driven the enemy a great distance, but had withdrawn. Emanuel Gentry having joined us, I sent G. back to tell our pickets we would go out & ascertain the enemy's position & not to shoot at us on returning.

The three of us after finding the Yanks in our old camp at New Market Heights returned and were going up the Darbytown road & were told by some women that a force of infantry had gone into the breastworks. Knowing we had captured the works I concluded of course they were our men, and rode right up to the breastworks where I found a great number of the troops. It was after midnight, but the moon was shining & by its light I saw the uniforms were dark. Harbin said, "Hey you fellows, what Reg't?" and one chap said, "44th Ohio!"

On my left was a company seated. At our horses' heads stood three Yanks & to the right were a number of skirmishers. Emanuel trotted at once to the rear of the skirmishers, when one chap said, "there's a skirmish line over there," and another suspecting us enquired our command, to which Harbin replied, "Ours is the 4th." "Oh, no," said the speaker, "You can't come that. Halt. hold."

---

7 These are the skirmishes and engagements of Darbytown and New Market Roads (October 7) and Chaffin's Farm (October 8).

I turned & ran down the road. Two men jumped at E.'s horse, one of whom was knocked down & trampled & the other hurt some way or other. Harbin instead of following me went with Emanuel, who escaped & H. must have been caught. Some 40 shots were fired at us hurriedly, but we (Emanuel & I) came out. I halted about 200 yards off & waited for H. to come, but not seeing or hearing anything of him we came away.

A long ride brought us to the Williamsburg road, where I found the 7th's pickets. My first enquiry, of course, was about Willie & I was considerably grieved to hear he was captured. The circumstances were these. Seeing some five or six Yanks ahead of him, he rode forward to capture them; they surrendered & were being brought in when Co. "G" was ordered to charge. Willie didn't hear the command & was thus separated from his Co. Shortly after a force of the enemy appeared in force in rear of the 7th which the prisoners saw & quietly turned taking Willie with them. His horse was captured also, and I am consequently in hopes they allowed him to take his blanket. As he was to be taken, I am glad the cavalry took him; they are a more genteel set than the infantry.

With a scant supply of clothes I am afraid he will suffer from the cold, as a decided change has occurred here in the past few days. God grant he may be well treated for much as he dislikes them, he wouldn't harm a prisoner for the world. I trust that the exchange may shortly be renewed.

I can say but little; our deeds are covered up by the misfortune that has befallen me. The Legion captured a U.S. flag, six pieces of artillery & about 150 horses & I who went on a horse raising expedition came back empty handed & missed the fight, tho' to say something about the latter — I missed it honorably & no blame is attached to me, but I must acknowledge my regrets at being absent.

[First] Sergt. [Daniel] Mitchell of Willie's Co. came to see me today.[8] *He bore with him the sympathies of the company & very generously gave me his brother-in-law's address that Willie might write him for assistance. It is Byron Ford, Clyde, Wayne County, New York. Fortunately I have $20 in greenbacks here & if I can*

---

8   Roster of the 7th South Carolina Cavalry (NA Microfilm, roll 47).

only hear from Willie can send it to him. I telegraphed Father yester-day about Willie & Frank & told him to write you.

God give us strength to bear up under the affliction & make us thankful his life is spared to us. Think of poor Mrs. Hughes, who has lost one son lately by death, another captured & a third whose life is suspended on a thread. God bless her is my prayer.

Gary & the cavalry received much credit for the part they bore in the action of Friday [October 7]. The 7th [South Carolina Cavalry] & our losses were comparatively few.

I am quite well, thank God & hope you are all enjoying the same inestimable blessing. Excuse my careless writing, as I am in much haste. Give much love to Annie, Carrie, Hattie, & Rob-bie. Kiss them all for me. Best love to Father and Sammie.

Lee is being heavily reinforced & glorious news comes to us over the wire tonight I learned. I hope it's true. My humble, earnest prayer is that God will bless us.

Most affectionately
Elliott

Hd. Qtrs. Hampton Legion
[Monday] October 24th 1864

Dear Father

It is a long time since I have written you & having a chance I'll now make amends for my delay.

One of the scouts from the 7th Cavalry took a Yankee recent-ly who upon being questioned said he saw a young rebel whose name he thought was Welch and described him. He was seen several days after the battle and was well. God grant it is so, tho' for myself I feel very well satisfied that he is safe.

We have but little news in Richmond, the latest from Early in the Valley is thought but little of — most people think we had the best of it save in the cannon. The Richmondites think of establishing a cannon foundry in the Valley to supply him.

[General Philip] Sheridan as usual blows supply lines up. He looks as though [2 words illegible] ...a second Julius Caesar and except as Bonaparte in his brilliant conceptions, and the sudden appearance of himself on the field "turned disaster into a splendid

victory." R. D. Ogden, the Henchman of Richmond, who ran away some time ago has been caught & has signed a suite of apartments in Castle Thunder.

One day last week I rode around the line of Hagood's Brigade with Gen. Lee's Staff, the Gen. being in front. On Wednesday night [October 19] Logan told me to accompany our band on a serenade to Gen. [James] Longstreet & represent the Legion as its Adjutant. I did the honors, had a long chat with Gen. L. & shook hands with him. I came away. He commands his old Corps in the Northside & we are temporarily under him.

This being Adjutant is a great thing & I hope it may continue so. So long as I had Frank Hughes it was a pleasure & you have no idea how much I miss him. Our reg't has lost one of its brightest ornaments & our company the brightest most talented man. The same evening Willie was captured I lost by capture a very intimate friend Arthur Harbin of Co. C, one of the scouts. He was taken at my side & I couldn't render any assistance; in fact it took all my tact to save myself.

I rode into a brigade of Yankees, near enough to shake hands with some of them thinking they were our own men. It wasn't till in reply to our query, "What reg't is this?" & they said, "44th Ohio!" that I was aware that our troops had retired from the works & they were occupied by the enemy. Being on a fleet horse I escaped with a comrade — their spirits went up. Some 30 or 40 shots were fired at us but didn't hurt anyone.

A few days before that I was sent to charge a picket post & a strong reserve of dismounted men was in rear. We drove them in but were in turn driven back by a superior force, losing two men wounded, one horse killed, & one wounded. Yankee loss unknown. I was on a white horse & was shot at a dozen times or more. Besides heavy artillery opened on us. I "fell back" in good order as usual on such occasions.

Last week on Thursday [October 20] we checked them [3 words are illegible] and knowing Logan would send me anywhere I went to Major [Benjamin E.] Nicholson who was commanding the Legion.[9]

---

9   Nicholson began the war as the 1st sergeant of Company B. He rose to 2nd lieutenant in August 1861 and 1st lieutenant in June 1862. In September of that year he became the company captain and then became the major in September 1864. On October 7, 1864 he was wounded on the Darbytown Road. He finished the war as the colonel.

(Simpson, 1977, 398)

Logan was acting Brig. but the Col. sent for me & told me to be A. Asst. Adj. Gen'l. and as such I was kept pretty busy most[ly] under fire. I had to lead the 47th Ala. into position while the Yankees were charging us. If allowed to do as I chose I'd have waited a while for the trenches were low & we had to go behind the line for a long distance. So thick were [the] bullets that the infantry broke. I expected every minute to be lifted out of my saddle but came out unhurt.

The man who rides with Logan into action must expect to go into hot places. He often sends a man unnecessarily, for instance, Frank Hughes — more caution is necessary & I hope he'll exhibit it particularly if I am with him.

Capt. [John D.] Palmer is still away & over his time.

[First Lieutenant William G.] Gardner is in camp but does no duty — his papers were approved for retirement by the Medical Board & are up for approval before the Sec. of War. Should my life be spared, as soon as he leaves I shall be promoted I suppose.

The horse you bought for me was captured & will prove a total loss, I am afraid. It is my attention to see Gen. [Martin W.] Gary about the matter however.[10]

I bought a very substantial horse recently for $500 & a furlough if'n I could get from 3 to $4000 for him, I think. Should I capture a horse, it will be property in the event of failure to get pay for "Frank."

This morning Col. [Thomas] Logan, Maj. [John C.] Haskell [in the C.S.A. artillery] & several other officers were trying the qualities of different pistols — the Colt's Army size was the best fortunately. I have a very fine one now & hope I shall live to keep it a long time.

Mother told me recently in a letter that you thought of quitting town. I hope you will, for I'm quite uneasy now that you are so low down to me i.e. for the range of shells; another reason is most of the soldiers with whom you did business have left & it hardly pays to stay in Camp.

We have lost [Second Sergeant] Willie [H.] Simmons one of our best and bravest members. [At Chaffin's Farm on September

---

10 Gary had been a general since June 1864.
(Evans, 1987, 396)

*29, 1864] he jumped upon the works & called out to his com-
rades to join him there as it was a splendid place to shoot from,
but before he could, he fell shot through the head. We soon after
fled the fortifications & I cannot tell where he lay or what became
of his body. I deeply sympathize with his poor Mother & sisters
— he was the only son of a widowed mother.*

*The weather is cold & wintry. I think we've had ice one of
these cold mornings of the past week.*

*Give my love to Mother, Annie, Carrie, Harry, Robbie when
you write. Love to Aunt Emily, Uncle William, Cousin Lauren &
family. Regards to Madam Favien, Mr. Darrill & enquiring friends.
I am very well & hope you are all enjoying the same great blessing. Love to Sammie, Mrs. Wightman & Maggie. God bless you
and reunite us speedily is my daily prayer. I shall write Sammie
shortly.*

*Your affectionate Son
Elliott*

*Head Quarters Hampton Legion
Williamsburg road
[Sunday] October 30th 1864*

My dear Mother,

*Annie's letter of the 22nd, yours of the 24th have both reached
me & for which accept my thanks. Again I have to record a fight
& again I am out safely thank God. Last Thursday [October 27],
just two weeks from the 13th we were aroused at 4 A.M. &
moved into the trenches — a large force of the enemy having been
reported crossing the James to our side. At seven A.M. skirmishing
commenced at the Darbytown road — we were on the Chas. City
[road], our works strengthened, abatis strong in a double line in
front and every man assigned to his place. At eight [A.M.] it began
in our front, but our rifle pits were too strong to be carried by skirmishers, & we in the trenches had no fight. At twelve [noon] we
were moved at the double quick to the Williamsburg road, where
the 24th Va. [Cavalry] held a good line of Yanks in check and the
infantry, coming over, we mounted our horses and went to the
Nine mile road at which point no enemy was to be found. After*

leaving the infantry an attack was made upon the Williamsburg road & we were galloped back, the assault was easily repulsed & while lying in the rain watching an artillery duel the yank's drove in our pickets on the Nine mile [road] & back we went.

On nearing the road we could hear orders given in the woods in front & started at a double quick, soon, before leaving the timber, they raised a yell & started for the works, which we had not reached, we then ran & it was a foot race for the point, we arrived first, but so close were the enemy & in such force, that we couldn't hold the works & artillery, tho' a cracked battery, fired so slowly that they ran over us, captured two guns & compelled us to leave the left of the line. Just at this time the 24th Va. [Cavalry] & 7th S.C. [Cavalry] came tearing up, yelling like demons & the portion of the Legion that retired returned, the <u>negroes</u> *took a pause & ran off. We retook the guns & fortifications.[11] Strange to say but one man of our whole brigade was killed — [First Corporal Oswell] Strohecker of Charleston (Co "A") & but one wounded — Col. [William Todd] Robins of the 24th Va. [Cavalry] slightly in the foot.[12]*

We were attacked by negroes who had never fought before — the Legion was the only regiment that shot at them & yesterday [Saturday, October 29] we sent a detail to bury their dead. One Col., Major, a Captain [William B. Clark, 22nd U.S. Colored Troop] & two other white officers [Captains Judson Rice and William W. Houston, 1st U.S. Colored Troop] & twenty three negroes were buried; five blacks were left unburied, making thirty three killed; several died of wounds the day after the fight.[13]

---

11   Captain Henry Ward and 15 enlisted men from the 1st U.S.C.T. were captured while trying to take the guns off the field.

Adjutant General's Office, *Official Army Register of the Volunteer Force of the United States Army*, Part VIII (Gaithersburg, MD: Ron R. Van Sickle Military Books, Reprint 1987), 169.

Robert Scott, (comp.), *The Official Records of the War of the Rebellion*, Vol. XLII, part 1 (Washington: U.S. Government Printing Office), 151, 816-817.

12   Strohecker died on the Nine Mile Road.

(Simpson, 1977, 403)

Robins had been wounded earlier that year by a falling tree (February) and then by a Federal bullet on June 14.

13   Elliott Welch erred somewhat in his report. The Confederates who retook the guns probably killed Captain Henry Ward (1st U.S.C.T. and his 15 men who tried to take the guns back into the Federal lines. They did kill a Dr. J. W. Mitchell (4th U.S.C.T.) who fell in the charge of the 1st U.S.C.T. Doctors held the rank of Major in the Feeral service. He was apparently on

Just before losing the artillery, Gen. Gary sent me to Gen. [Charles William] Field [C.O., Hood's old division] for reinforcements & I galloped my horse all the way to the Williamsburg road, three miles & failing to find him, I rode to the works, where our skirmish line was taking some prisoners & saw a man lying down; he asked me if I were an officer; on giving him my rank he said, "Well Sir, I'll surrender my sword to you then!" and handed me his saber. He gave me his address Lt. Col. R. M. Strong, 19th Wisconsin Infantry. He was shot in the leg. So a Col. has given up to your boy. His whole brigade surrendered, i.e. what was left of them. Bratton's & the Texas brigades took 500 prisoners, seven flags & a quantity of rifles, besides innumerable oil clothes, etc. I have a splendid blanket, which I suppose belonged to some negro mother.

During the night they left & in the morning [October 28] we followed them but with the exception of a few stragglers nothing could be seen save the <u>debris</u> of their extra luggage, which they destroyed.

Nothing yet from Willie, but I think the cause of it [is that] there have been no flag of truce boats up the river since his removal from City Point, which took place about a week after his capture I suppose. I am anxious to know something about him, tho' as yet [I] feel no hesitancy in saying that he is safe. God bless & protect him is my daily prayer.

Frank, my darling friend, is the greatest loss to me. In everything I miss him. Oh I pray that his dear Mother may have strength to bear up under her heavy afflictions. A brave, noble, generous youth was Frank H[ughes]. I feel that he is happier, and better off than we. Mr. Taylor — Frank's brother in law — wrote to a friend in New York to supply Toni Hughes with whatever he stood in need of.

---

the staff of Major General Godfrey Weitzel and the rolls show one staff officer missing. The records show only the three officers cited in the text as fatalities for that day.

The 1st U.S.C.T. lost 2 officers killed; 4 officers wounded; 1 officer captured; 10 men killed; 92 men wounded; 15 captured.

The 22nd U.S.C.T. lost 1 officer killed; 1 officer wounded; 4 men killed; 44 men wounded.
The 37th U.S.C.T. lost 1 officer wounded; 1 man wounded.
Total casualties 17 killed; 143 wounded; 16 missing.

Welch accounted for 33 dead Federals, which equals exactly the number of men reported killed or missing and the number who were known dead among the black troops.

A.G.O., Part VIII 1987, 169, 193)
OR, Vol. XLII, part 1, 151, 814-820)

Last night [October 29] I asked Col. [Thomas] Logan if he would receive Sammie into the regiment without a horse & he said "Oh yes, we can easily get a horse for him." I told him Sammie would fight to which he replied "I know that." So should you get Father's consent to come out, tell him to wait awhile and I shall see what my chances are for a furlough when things quiet down & he can come back with me (P.V.) if I get off.

[Captain John D.] Palmer has returned — came back just in time to run up to the Nine mile road & get in the fight. He looks well. [First Lieutenant William G.] Gardner's papers haven't yet returned, but we look daily for them.

I hope sincerely Father has determined to quit business and Mr. Harris, in Charleston.[14] I wrote him recently & hinted at the matter — hope he'll take the hint. I owe Sammie & Carrie each a letter & must write, should nothing happen, tomorrow to them.

I have been unable to go as far up as the Jackson Hospital when I've been in town & consequently have never seen Mr. Atkinson — should I be able to go there any day I'll try to find him. I haven't had a chance of calling on my friend Miss Walker since Frank's death & in fact have not had the clothes to do so in. Ask Annie if she has a pair of socks please to send them to me. I never could think of it when I wrote. I drew two pairs today, but they are worsted & I prefer cotton — perhaps I'd better keep them for Father — they are English, tho' coarse. I hope our new clothes will come soon. If I get behind the Yankee lines it would be easy to get a whole suit save a jacket.

[Tuesday] Nov. 1st. Dark coming on last Sabbath I was unable to finish & yesterday we had a regular two months' muster & inspection which kept me busy nearly all day. For any one to be around Col. [Thomas] Logan he must expect to "fly around" somewhat, which in times of a small stir prevents letter writing almost to a certainty. Take the will for the deed & I'll write whenever the opportunity presents itself.

I am rather disappointed in my horse trade, tho' not jockeyed in the least. For draft purposes my Konistoga can't be beaten, but he is dreadfully rough for saddle purposes. As soon as I can I shall take him to town & trade or sale him.

---

14   I could not identify this Mr. Harris.

Last night [October 31] I asked Col. Logan for another furlough to give some man for a horse & offered to dispose of mine at a very low figure, to which he consented, so that if I fail to get a good price I can fall back on that offer (P.V.). I am now going to play "honest sharper" & see if I can get a horse for Sammie — one that will stand service well & being allowed to keep two horses, can keep him at Hd Qrs. as long as I remain here or Sammie comes on. I intend to speak to Palmer shortly about trading off some of Co. "H" to the infantry for a few good men, but if he refuses & Sammie comes I'll get him before Co. "A" learns more of that hereafter.

[U.S.] Grant appears satisfied with his recent reconnaissances & is lying quiet, tho' we were up at daylight & saddled. Tell Annie my giving a furlough to a man for a horse doesn't prevent my furlough's being granted when the leaves of absence are recommended.

The weather is glorious — clear & cold. I am quite well for which blessing I am still very thankful. Should nothing happen I'll try a trip tomorrow. Much love to Annie, Carrie, Harry & Robbie. Kiss them for me. Send love to Father & Sammie. Kind regards to Mrs. Keith & family & all enquiring friends. God bless you all with health, and reunite us is my constant prayer.

Your affectionate Son,
Elliott

Hd. Qrs. Hampton Legion
[Wednesday] November 16th 1864

My dear Mother,

Your kind letter of the 9th & 11th came duly to hand, one enclosing a note from Annie, the other one from Carrie. The letter I see was directed in Carrie's hand. Accept my thanks for all, to Sis particularly; she only wants practice & confidence to do well.

I have been trading horses and think I've done well. I have given my Konestoga & 40 day furlough for a beautiful mare & 1200 dollars. I was not entitled to the furlough, but taking some of the money I shall buy a horse & present him to a dismounted man, which act will give me a furlough for an enlisted man. The *horse I shall buy & present to Sammie who will come into our company & thus I shall be benefitted by the transaction. This is my plan. My new horse is lame in one foot from hard riding & the trade was if at all affected by the strain, the bargain was to be worked. Do you think I've done well in my second horse trade.*

[Thursday] 17th. It was too cold to finish last night & being very busy all day I have resumed by candle light. Yesterday was thanksgiving & we had service by the Rev. Mr. Johnston, missionary to the 7th S.C.[15] *He is a splendid speaker & much admired by all who hear him. His remarks [were] about the state of the country and comparing the state of it with the state of our souls. His views were lucid & very appropriate. As yet we haven't heard our old friend Mr. Grier — dear though the few Charleston men in the regt. are very anxious to see & hear him.*[16]

I saw a young man of the 7th who says he saw the letter from Mr. Sheler which stated that Willie was well & at Point Lookout two weeks ago.[17] *I hope you have heard from him ere this. Poor Mrs. Hughes has again met with a great loss — her youngest daughter Lizzie, a sweet girl of sixteen. On the reception of the news of Frank's death, she exposed herself somehow & took a severe cold, changing to hasty consumption & ending in death. Dear Mrs. Hughes, three of her jewels have been transplanted in the Heavenly crown, while one is in a Yankee dungeon. Truly she is deeply afflicted. (Miss Sallie wrote Auld & said she feared her Mother could not survive the shock.)*

We have started in downright earnest to prepare winter quarters and as soon as they are finished I presume we shall change our quarters & either lie out in the cold or build again. Col. [Thomas] Logan has selected Capt. [E. Scott] Carson [Company G] to superintend the erection of the stables & has appointed me to <u>superintend</u> *Carson.*[18] *I hope we shall soon get thro'. Logan*

15   I could not identify this individual.

16   George W. Grier (age 32) was a merchant in Ward 6 of Charleston. He supported his wife, Mary E. (age 28) and a daughter, Carrie L. (age 5).
Entry for George W. Grier, Charleston County, SC, Census for Population, (NA Microfilm, roll 1216, 416) Records of the Census, 1860, MA, South Carolina.

17   Sheler is unidentified.

18   Carson began the war as a first corporal and made captain of his company by April 1, 1864. He was paroled at Farmville in April 1865.
(Simpson, 1977, 443)

will make a pretty good officer & Adjutant of me if I remain long enough with him. Palmer remarked today he intended to get me in a position where I shall rise to the Captaincy & then resign in my favor. Should he do so I hope my life may be spared to be a blessing to all around me. I've been urging Palmer to see Gary about getting command of the Horse artillery to be attached to our brigade. Longstreet has given us four guns & we are to furnish men & horses. Should I succeed, I'll bend all my energies to the task of fitting out, studying & drilling for active service. Should I be successful, I think I'd fight artillery as it is fought by few: at close range.

I love the branch of service and should do all in my power to render it a science. But tho' almost an enthusiast on the subject, I have no hopes of accomplishing it. Logan will say No! when we ask him to give us the guns & that will be the end of it. Some day when he is in a good humor I'll speak of the matter to him & know his decision will be "Old Mart's". ["Mart" refers to Brigadier General Martin W. Gary.]

We have no news at all today from any quarter, as there were no papers this morning. I am a thousand times obliged for the pantaloons you sent & to Annie for the socks. If the trousers fit me I'll surely keep them as I am still in a pair of borrowed ones & our clothing is still in the Qr. master's storehouse. I recently went to town to purchase a pair & was treated with indifference by a few upstart clerks that I felt like flogging them. It was rainy weather & after wishing them, very piously that the Conscript officers might take them & send them to the front, I left.

If nothing happens tomorrow I shall probably go to town to see after some little affairs & shall try to go the Jackson Hospital where I hope to see Mrs. Atkinson. I am still enjoying excellent health & thank God for the great blessing. I hope you all continue well. Am glad to hear that you are so frisk & that Annie has improved. Much love to Father & Sammie for me. Kiss Annie, Carrie, Harry & Robbie for me & give kindest regards to all enquiring friends.

God bless you dear mother & all and may He answer our prayers for dear Willie's safety & return.

Your affectionate boy
Elliott

The following is Samuel B. Welch's only 1864 letter in this collection. He was 17 at the time.

> *Camp of the 8th Batt. Columbia, S.C.*
> *[Thursday] Nov. 24th 1864*

My Dear Mother

You'll be greatly surprised I've no doubt to receive a letter from me at this place but having been ordered here in a hurry I hadn't time to acquaint you from Charleston.

We left the "City by the Sea" [Charleston, S.C.] last Tuesday morning [November 22] at 2 a.m. & arrived here Wednesday night [November 23] at 7 P.M. after a journey of 30 or 40 hours on the road, going a distance of 130 miles. On the route I suffered exceedingly from the cold, we being in an old deteriorated box car, with holes & cracks at every turn which let in the cold wind in perfect streams. Now we are just outside of this town awaiting wagons to transport our baggage to camp.

We have a very pleasant place here but can't stay long. Should our future camp be as pleasant as this I for one will be content. I have the Capt's. boy cooking for me, & expect to fare very well. I came off in a hurry & forgot to bring a plate & knife & fork but can borrow them from some of the men, until I hear from my application. It has been sent to the Sec. of War & will probably be kept a week longer by him, but when it does come, if approved by him, I'll drop in & give you a call.

Do write me if Ellie comes home, & for how many days & if my application is not heard from, I'll ask to be transferred & get a 30 day furlough to report in, which time I can spend at home & then go out with Ellie. Don't forget to write.

The wagons have just come & I must close, will write you from the new camp. Direct your letters to S. B. Welch, Capt. [William H.] Bartless's Co., 8th Batt. Reserves, Columbia.[19]

Love to My Annie, Carrie, Harry. Kiss Robbie for me.

I get rations plenty but should I want any thing will write you about [it]. Am writing on my Knee, so you excuse this scrawl. Write soon.

> *Your affectionate Son*
> *Sammie*

---

19   Roster of the 8th Battalion South Carolina Reserves (NA Microfilm, roll 234), NA.

Hd. Qrs. Hampton Legion
[Sunday] November 27th 1864

My dear Mother,

For the life of me, 'tis about impossible for me to decide whether I'm on my head or my feet — I have in my pocket a furlough for 25 days and do you believe I have concluded to remain with the reg't. till about the 15th of Dec. in order to spend Christmas, New Year's Day & my birthday [at home] — does this arrangement suit you?

This afternoon I told [Captain John D.] Palmer I had rec'd my furlough and had decided to remain till next month, when [he] jumped up & said, "I wish you let me have it then, my wife's very ill," or thinking I wouldn't do that he changed his tune & said he wished I['d] come back & take the company, as he'd like to go home for about ten days. I consented very reluctantly, but made him understand that if his furlough came back approved & he failed to report to the company, I should go off & leave it. His remark may be true & it may be one of his flank movements to get home & stay there; at all events he can't dispossess me of my papers.

Yesterday [November 26] we had a brigade review by "Old Mart." It was quite a grand affair and in the presence of the whole command & spectators, I had a terrible fall — horse & self. Fortunately the ground was soft & I wasn't hurt more than a little bruise; my horse went to jump two ditches at once, but plunging in the second, both of us went down; I was riding very fast with Logan around the line at the time of the "upset." Such is War!

The review was a decided success. [Brigadier General Martin W.] Gary with a flashy uniform & a gaudily dressed staff flourished extensively on the field. After the review, I went to town & rode to the Jackson Hospital and afterward went to see Miss Walker, with whom & several other young ladies I spent a very pleasant evening till someone proposed a game of dominoes & then I was almost bored to death. I made several ineffectual efforts to "turn the tune" & gave up in despair. I shall call again, if I am spared, before starting for home. Miss Lizzie [Walker] is a splendid girl. Her brother, who was captured on his trip from his home to our lines last Spring, returned — he is only about six feet six in his stockings. My trip to Jackson Hospital was unsuccessful. I could neither find Mrs. Atkinson nor my bundle.

Annie's letter of the 16th came this evening. Mr. A. mailed it on the 20th in Richmond. I have rec'd a note from him & as his camp is near ours I shall go tomorrow & see him and probably get my package; its contents on a home trip would be very acceptable indeed.

Last Wednesday evening [November 23] Col. [Thomas M.] Logan was in town & wrote me a note requesting the band to come to the city to serenade some friends for him. The weather had been remarkably cold & damp, but toward sunset appeared to brighten somewhat, the stars coming out after nightfall. Notwithstanding the cold, we started. I was rolled in my overcoat, my feet in a blanket & a warm pair of gloves on & consequently thought my chance for keeping warm very good. When near town it commenced to snow, having clouded up again as we were driving and became so intensely cold that we had to go to Maj. [William H.] Mauldin [A.Q.M. for the brigade] and warm fires to our return. The party didn't reach the city. We knew no one could expect us on such a wild night & therefore [we] trotted back "double quick." It seemed as though I would never get my feet warm again, but fortunately a warm fire restored me.

I have my office nicely fixed up & a good chimney of brick and altogether very comfortable. Nicely arranged for a successor. We are now working at our stables & shall probably have them finished on Monday; the sooner the better, as there is a prospect of rain or snow very soon, tho' for the past three days we have had beautiful, bright sunshiny days.

So bright indeed that Gen. Lee suspected an advance from Grant and has had us preparing for it, tho' in a very quiet way. The Yankees have an idea we're part of a heavy force to check Sherman, and may accordingly attempt another "On to Richmond" which will surely come to grief.

My mare was injured by the fall yesterday & has a swollen ankle, which I hope will soon be well. Never until recently have I realized what a valuable horse I lost when Frank was captured. I've ridden many since that time, but haven't met with one to compare with him — I'd give a thousand dollars now for him instead of buying another horse.

Mother do you know I've several times thought of something again. Time passes so slowly and there's so little to render camp

73

life attractive that I am induced to speak to you of it. Unless I have your consent I shall not begin again; and then too the idea of getting every pretty girl I became acquainted with makes me a tobacco bag, which little things oftentimes gives one an insight into a lady's character — all these little matters help to persuade me to try again but just as you say.

I intended writing you last night and congratulating you and Father upon your 23rd wedding anniversary. Dear Parents, I hope & pray God will bless and spare you to see and enjoy a [new year] with all your children well & around you. We have many blessings and mercies to be thankful for. I pray God to bless us & restore dear Willie to us.

Tell Annie if she doesn't stop provoking me about chicken pies, etc. I'll — well there's no knowing what I'll do.

I am quite well now and hope you all are enjoying the same great blessing. Excuse the careless manner in which I've written. Send much love to Father and Sammie. Kiss Annie, Harry & Robbie for me. Kindest regards to all enquiring friends. Write me as soon as possible and accept much love from [me].

Your affectionate son,
Elliott

Chapter Four

THE CLOSING DAYS OF THE WAR (1865)

Early in 1865 Samuel B. Welch, age 17, joined the Legion but was never entered upon the books, a not too uncommon occurrence throughout the war. Elliott apparently traveled to Timmonsville, South Carolina to bring his brother north.

> *Hd. Qrs. Hampton Legion*
> *[Saturday] February 4th 1865*

Dear Father,

As Sammie has already written you I suppose he has given you a detail of our trip, which regarding delays and cold weather was anything but agreeable. I returned first in time and after telling Logan the cause of my delay he inquired if I was prepared to resume my duties in the office and on telling him I desired it, I was, he told me, to go to work. Lt. [John T.] Donaldson [Company D] did pretty well I suspect but I found a great want of system and in the absence of the Sergt. Major [James H. Ancrum] find my hands quite full. [1]

Before this Mother has told you I suppose of my having three letters from Willie. I sent them home; have sent Willie some money and shall send some clothes and tobacco at the first chance. He was very well. Wasn't it strange that the first tidings of him should be received on his birthday? That old fortune teller's word was true about hearing of him — wonder which of us is to be wounded now.

---

1 Donaldson began the war as a private.
Ancrum left the Legion in July 1864 to become a second lieutenant in the artillery.
(Simpson, 1977, 399, 423)

Last night [February 3] I wrote a long letter to Annie & shall probably do so tomorrow for Mother. About 2 o'clock this morning an order came to camp to look out for Yankees, so I couldn't go to town today as I contemplated and shall have to wait till Monday before being able to see to shipping Willie's things.

What is Sherman doing? Are you going to let him take Charleston or not? Our papers here say he's within thirty miles of Branchville & going on. Gen. Lee is now in supreme command, and says he sees nothing to cause alarm.

We had a Mass War Meeting here last Thursday [February 2] & I was chairman. After stating the object of the meeting, Adj. [Beaufort W.] Ball spoke; resolutions were passed, then [Thomas M.] Logan, [1st Lieutenant James] McElroy [Company A] & [Colonel George B.] Crittenden spoke.[2] I was too hoarse to speak or I might have given our men a war talk. It was passed that the resolution be published in the S.C. papers, so you will probably see our doings. It was a unanimous thing and though but little enthusiasm was manifested there was a quiet determination to "stick it out." McElroy's speech took best of all. I made a friend of Ball for life by introducing him as "a talented and distinguished member of the H.L." He thanked me for the compliment & will sign passes innumerable, no doubt.

Logan's commission as Brigadier hasn't come yet, tho' Butler has lately asked for him and wants him. We can't very well afford to lose him. Our men are doing duty on foot and have couriers mounted to accompany them. It is a great saving of horse flesh and by Spring if we got reinforcements we shall have quite a fine lot of horses. My mare was in a horrible fix when I returned but by careful attention, she will come out.

We are getting short rations of meat & bacon, with a little rice & peas. Under this diet, Sammie's coming down a little and will weight by Spring about 140. He is well and sends much love to

---

2   Beaufort started the war as a private in Company B. McElroy was also a private at the beginning of the war.

(Simpson, 1977, 399, 402)

Crittenden, a former brigadier general, served on the staff of Brigadier General John S. Williams as an unofficial colonel.

Stewart Sifakis, *Who Was Who in the Civil War*, (Facts on File Publications: New York, 1988), 151-152.

you. Accept my love. Love to Mrs. Wightman & Maggie, Uncle
W., Aunt E. & family, Cousin Laura & family & all enquiring friends.
I am at present very well; hope your health is good. Regards to
Madam Favico & Mr. [James] Darrill.[3] God bless you Father is the
prayer of Your affectionate Son,

Elliott

Camp Hampton Legion
[Thursday] February 9th 1865

My Dear Mother

Your welcome letter of the 1st inst. was rec'd by us this morning & you can scarcely conceive the joy we felt at its reception.
Glad to hear that you are well & that Miss Annie has recovered
from her last indisposition.

Everything remains in status quo around our settlement & is
likely to remain so as long as the present bad weather continues.
Yesterday morning [February 8] early it commenced snowing,
sleeting & hailing & kept it up until about 12 noon at which time
it varied a little & started to rain. This was kept up until evening
& you will judge in what a predicament it left the ground, which
was very muddy before, but which was left much more so by this
new addition. In the immediate vicinity of our tent the mud was
about ankle deep and in the road it will reach our knees or
waist. This is caused of course by the frequent passage of horses
& wagons of which there are a considerable number in & around
our camp & the road will hardly be better as long as the winter lasts.

As bad as the weather is out of doors it affects us but slightly
in our nice & comfortable abode & if you wish to see a contrast
step in & we will exhibit it.

To a new & very commodious wall-tent is added that great
desired item — a chimney, in which at the present moment blazes

---

3   Madam Favico remains unidentified.

James Darrill (age 44), an Irish born laborer, lived in the same Charleston Ward as the Welch's.
He lived with his wife, Mary (age 39) and their 4 children: John (age 16), Mary (age 13), Jane
(age 17), and Ellen (age 9).

Entry for James Darrill, Charleston County, SC, Census of Population (NA Microfilm, roll
1216, 204) Records of the Census, 1860, SC.

a warm & cheerful looking fire. Opposite the chimney rests our bed or rather bunk which was made for Ellie by some of the men and which accommodates 3 occupants nicely & might by dint of a little pressure be made to take in 4. To all this is added a very good floor elevated about 3 or 4 inches from the earth & which we find very comfortable for it keeps our feet warm & also prevents the rain & water from getting to us. Around the hearth (we have one) sit several stools & these are constantly occupied if not by ourselves by visitors from different portions of the regiment who call in to hear the news & to know the topics of the day; for remember, it is the Adjutant's tent & the place where rumours gain circulation & truths become known.

Ellie is quite a favorite in the regiment & of course his friends must call in occasionally to see him & this together with his duties as Adj. account for the number of visitors.

The culinary department is conducted under the supervision of Mr. James Pusick with about half [a] dozen negroes as "instruments," who do the cooking etc. for Head Qrs.[4] His department is excellently arranged & does great credit to Mr. P. for the manner in which he carries it on. We have of course but two meals a day — breakfast at about 10 [A.M.] & dinner at 4 or 5 [P.M.] & as a sample of what we get I will tell you that yesterday morning we had sausages, wheat biscuit, bacon, ham, corn bread & coffee & sugar. For dinner [we had] boned turkey, rice, cabbage, boiled ham, fried ditto & corn bread. This morning roast sparrows, sausages, ham, etc. The sparrows we catch in abundance since the snow fell & some of the other things were sent from home to one of the mess. Though we always get good rations & live high generally. Don't feel any concern on our account, for the authorities know how to feed the Army of Northern Virginia & though I have fed on musle [mussel] and molasses, & may have to do so again, I'm not doing it now nor will I be forced to unless there is a very material change in any prospect of our affairs a calamity which I trust may never occur.

Yesterday Dick Parham got some things from home and last night about 9 P.M. we had a supper after all which is obsolete in

---

4   Pusick remains unidentified.

the army but which we thought to revive for the occasion at least.[5] We got a frying pan, fried some sauges [sic], made an egg omelet (the best we could), had some good wheat biscuits & then eat — & I can assure it was really excellent. Went to bed soon after and dreamed of hobgoblins, spirits, etc. & the likes but they didn't bother me in the least & I didn't bother them. Tonight if nothing prevents [us] we'll have a repetition of last night's work and I wish you were here to help us enjoy our good things.

Wood is not any plentiful in our immediate neighborhood, though by walking a short distance we are supplied very bountifully. Yesterday we turned out & cut an enormous oak tree down & I guess it will last us throughout the winter. We (i.e. Dick, Ellie & myself) have quite a pile of it now in our tent & whenever this stack is exhausted, we will go & cut more.

I am very much pleased with Va. & would like to live here though of course this is impossible, but I would like to make acquaintances & get in the good graces of the people for I know they are very kind & hospitable & it would probably pay to favor their friendship. I must confess that I am very agreeably disappointed at my treatment & fare for I expected to have a terribly rough time here, but if I were anywhere else than at home, I couldn't be better situated and I assure you that I wouldn't exchange places with any Quartermaster's clerk in the country unless he were stationed in Timmonsville, S.C. My only objection to Va. is the weather which is very cold, though I haven't felt much of it nor will I until I get on picket which will be in about a week or ten days' time.

Tomorrow [February 10] Ellie, Dick, myself & some others intend going to Richmond to hear [Confederate Vice President Alexander H.] Stephens & others speak & we anticipate a treat. I will write you an account if I go for it is to be a tremendous affair.

The peace mission has failed & just as I thought it would. Our people now see what we are to expect & I trust they may move their energies to the struggle & prepare for a more vigorous campaign than any we have yet had for when it does come it will be a terrible one & one in which all who are able should participate,

---

5   He is not listed on the rolls of Hampton's Legion or the 7th South Carolina Cavalry.

and I earnestly trust it may be decisive & finally end the war. To this end we should all pray, for through prayer only will we accomplish one object.

Having said my say I will now close. Do write me all the news. How are you off for provisions & have they raised any in T. (The price I mean) Did Father get any more cotton-cards? I think you had better lay in a stock of something of the sort in order to exchange for provisions.

Our brassband is playing just in front of our tent & I can't write. Excuse my errors & bad writing. Ellie says he'll write on Friday.

Much love to Sisters Annie & Carrie, Father, Harry & Robbie. Remember me to Mrs. Keith, McKay, Maurina, Mary & all. Write soon & often.[6] May God ever bless & protect you, dear Mother.

Your Affectionate Son
Sammie

Camp Hampton Legion
[Tuesday] Feb. 14th 1865

My Dear Mother,

Your very welcome & interesting letter was received by us a few days since & was answered by Ellie yesterday or the day before. Today I will take my turn and trust it may reach you, though the R.R. companies here are as much interrupted that I fear my exertions will be for nothing & that this epistle will never be forwarded to its destination. I will ask if you have [news of] the rest of the movements of Sherman.

As I wrote you in my last [letter] I went to Richmond to attend the mass meeting held on last Thursday [February 9], but unfortunately was unable to get in on account of the tremendous crowd in attendance. From those who heard the speeches I was told that they were really beautiful & worth the trouble of squeezing

---

6   Mr. Benjamin McKay (age 44) lived in Lynchburg, South Carolina about 30 miles west of Timmonsville. Dorothy McKay, his wife (age 44) had 5 children: Mary L. (age 15), Joseph R. (age 15), Ann E. (age 10), John M. (age 8), and Susan H. (age 6).

Entry Benjamin McKay, Sumpter County, SC, Census of the Population (NA Microfilm, roll 1227, 226), Records of the Census, 1860, South Carolina.

in to hear. Benjamin's speech or rather various extracts from it are quoted in our camp up to the present time and it is regarded by the H.L. to be perfection in the way of elocution. Stephens had started for him on Wednesday & consequently didn't attend. The audience expressed much disappointment on knowing that he had left for Georgia, as many who were there had come for the express purpose of hearing his <u>say</u> in relation to the Peace mission to Fortress Monroe. Their dissatisfaction, however, was not of long duration for Mr. Benjamin supplied his place & proved himself an excellent substitute. I was very sorry I didn't hear him for though it was utterly impossible to squeeze through the jam, and I had to give up in despair.

After leaving, Ellie & I roamed around the Capital & saw the sights after which E. visited some ladies & we then returned to camp, having spent quite an agreeable time, though we did miss the speaking.

There is nothing new in this vicinity all minds being absorbed by the news from So. Ca. everyone in the reg't. I believe, being more or less interested. Today we hear that Orangeburg has been burnt, Branchville captured & Charleston evacuated. There is nothing official in it that I know of, but you can judge of my feelings at the mention of it & that in South Carolina Sherman may receive a check a check which will necessitate a withdrawal of his forces from the state & leave our folks in the peaceful possession of their homes.

Ellie sent you $30 in greenbacks, which if you get [them] may be useful, for if the Yanks reach T. they will in all probability take all you have & this money may be the means of purchasing something from them which will keep you going until better times. Ma, if the Yanks should happen to reach Timmonsville (God grant they may not) I'd advise you to hide your stock of provisions, put on a bold face & threaten to shoot the first scoundrel who puts his foot on the threshold of your door. Sister Annie I guess will be the one to fix them & by being positive, it may be the means of saving all your eatables. Don't think for an instant of entertaining any of the villains, though this is a needless injunction for I know you'll not, dear mother, & should any of them intrude or go rummaging

81

around the place, don't hesitate to shoot. Show them no mercy for you'll receive none & by all means don't surrender any of your provisions.

Do write if you can and let me know your intentions, also those of Father. Don't trouble yourself about us for we are well provided for; my only desire being to know that you are doing well & likely to keep on until this cruel war closes, which God grant may be soon.

We see by the papers that arrangements have been completed to exchange all the prisoners at the rate of 3,000 a week & we may soon have the glorious satisfaction of seeing Willie return to us which will be quite an event in our little family circle & I trust will soon occur. With the addition of our released prisoners to the army we may hope for numerous successes this spring & by God's will & blessing we may obtain peace by next winter.

Today is the anniversary of St. Valentine, & there are several fellows around me writing to their "Pretty's," but I am one of the number who don't imbibe & I will celebrate the occasion by writing to you, which will afford me more pleasure than indicting "soft expressions" & still softer maybe "dulcies."

The weather has been quite cold for several days back, but today it is moderate. The mail carrier has come & I must close. Will try to write Sister A. in a day or two. Love to all.

> God bless & protect you
> Your affectionate Son
> Sammie

> Hd. Qrs. Hampton Legion
> [Saturday] February 18th 1865

My dear Mother,

What joy and what sorrow are mingled together in one single day, yes, in one short hour. Last Thursday night [February 16], a young man came over to my tent and told me Willie had come; that he was at Camp Lee and desired to see me. Yesterday morning [February 17] I borrowed a horse and with Sammie rode beyond Richmond to Camp Lee in a cold, rain, mud half leg deep and everything as bitterly opposed to travel, fast as could be. Leaving Sammie with the horses, I walked thru' an immense building

& peered into every face, but no evidence could be seen of him. Of the S.C. soldiers present none could tell me where he was. I rode to all gatherings of men and asked if Welch of the 7th S.C. Cav. was present but I was told "No" or had the cold shoulder turned on me. Returning to the main building I determined to try again and entering I shouted out, "Is there a man named Welch from S.C. here," when to my surprise, to my joy & concerning earthly happiness Willie ran up and took me by the hand — the same old Willie, only thinner and with a careworn expression on his otherwise, bright, handsome face. But a few minutes sufficed to have him in my overcoat and mounted on the horse I had brought for him and our ride tho' a cold one was passed, full of thankfulness for his safe deliverance and return. His "Five months among the Yankees at Point Lookout" was vividly described and as eagerly swallowed by two who love him well.

He has just returned to Camp for his furlough, which I hope he'll get and ere this reaches you but welcomed back among and by the loved ones at home. He has a cough which I'd not like and trust he may soon be rid of [it], otherwise his health is very good.

This is the happy picture — the one of sorrow is to think that Sherman is devastating our beloved State and with the "red hand of ruin" scattering devastation far and near. Do our people tamely submit or does the fire brand do its work to prevent his troops from feasting on our supplies? Mother dear, apply the torch before one of his dastardly followers has acquired from your larder. "'Tis sweet to die for one's country," has said a patriot and we can but die. Better to live on a crust and have contentment therewith than to share an abundance with such vile wretches as our enemies have proven themselves.

Our sins are numerous and our Heavenly Father is afflicting us with a dreadful punishment for our crimes but I feel that all will yet be well. Did I feel less faith in our ultimate success, or did I think hearts less brave than yours were home, I'd feel faint hearted myself but He who doeth all things well is guiding our destiny and in His hands I feel assured our cause will be well cared for.

To me, the most serious objection of Sherman's occupation of S.C. is that my much loved letters will be stopped; but for our safety, I need hardly say entrust us to the care of Him, who has thus far protected us from <u>all</u> harm, and tho' it may be our lot to meet no more on earth, in Heaven we shall be reunited, when wars and separations are never known.

Do not think I am sad and "blue;" the former I am touched with <u>only</u> slightly, the latter not at all. But I must acknowledge I am greatly provoked to think that base villain is marching thro' our State without opposition. Why didn't the men fight? fight, I repeat. Is it because they are afraid, I wonder, and won't? If they would only send us where we could meet a few of his hordes, they would find out what Longstreet's men are composed of. Fight, I say — men, women, and children ought to show them hatred — their eternal hatred (not fear) of everything Yankee.

I never was over brave but I have preserved my name so far, I believe, with a clear showing, this campaign. I shall endeavor to do something more, — rest assured, 'twill be nothing rash or foolish but my duty and so much more as possible.

Well don't think I design devoting all my letter to writing an "editorial" in a war sermon, but my thoughts mutually went to home in these "troubled times," and a little anxiety felt to know how you are getting on.

About a week ago, fearing the enemy might get in your neighborhood I sent you all the "greenbacks." I had some $30 which I hope has reached you ere this time. Willie having returned to Dixie, I am desirous of your retaining it as it will be useful.

Last Tuesday night [February 14] I took the band into town to serenade some friends and of course gave my friend Miss Walker and the Misses Rahin the benefit of it. Mr. Rahin (a fine young man & brother of the ladies) invited us in and had a fine collation provided for us.[7] I was sorry he put himself to the trouble for nothing was expected but, as 'twas there, we had to do justice to it, or give offense & I am satisfied all felt as tho' no ill feelings should be rec'd from our actions. After the music the family insisted on us remaining all night which I did <u>not</u> feeling even incl[ined].

A standing invitation has been extended for me to go on one Sunday to church & dinner afterwards. How heartless it seems for

---

7   Rahin remains unidentified.

anyone to participate in any gayety when our homes much times from associations and those that dwell there may be a heap of ruins lying in ashes and those to whom our thoughts went fleeing before a victorious army, or compelled to remain among them and be subjects of every insult imaginable. The only excuse I shall offer as a palliative is we have become so hardened from witnessing such scenes every day that they fail to excite to some extent our fairness and finer feelings and sympathies.

And the next step 'tis said will be to send a force around and cut off Charleston by way of Bull's Bay. Well let it go but even then we are far from being whipped. As in the revolution our country may be overrun but we shall come out yet "right side up with care." I think Sherman will find himself in a snap one of these fine mornings from which 'twill [be] hard to extricate himself.

19th. Last night Willie returned to camp having rec'd a furlough and found he couldn't leave till tonight so I decided to send all my letters by him and answer up all my correspondents. Friday morning I rec'd a letter from Annie. I am much pleased you have found such pleasant neighbors as in Mrs. [illegible], McL. & Mrs. B. very little evidence. Present my regards to them if they have not become alarmed and left S.C.

We have no news in camp at all, everything is considerably quiet, save the usual artillery that occurs at the Gap. Our chaplain Mr. Fleming has returned & we may now expect a resumption of religious services in camp, a body of religious men without a guide is like a rabble without a leader they can't get along well.[8] I am glad he is back. The leader of our band has not yet returned & I am constrained to think he has been pressed into service in S.C.

I hope you are well and that your headaches have entirely disappeared.

[Wednesday] 22nd & [Thursday] 23rd.

Willie will endeavor to drive them away from you. Sammie & I are very well with the exception of slight colds. Hoping our communications will not be interfered with, Your affectionate Sons.

Elliott

---

8 Fleming is unidentified.

Much love to Annie, Carrie, Harry & Robbie. Kiss them all for me. Where is Father? I acknowledge feeling much concern about him. Love to all. Regards to friend.

> Camp Hampton Legion
> [Friday] Feby. 24th 1865

My Dear Mother,

Your very interesting and welcomed letter of the 18th inst. reached us this morning, together with others from yourself & Sister, Annie to Ellie and you have little idea of the joy they created in our bosoms on learning that you were all well in health & spirits, that amid the excitement and terror which pervades our State you are unmoved and continue to pursue the even tenor of your ways, believing in our ability to whip the enemy, and trusting in a higher Power to bring about our deliverance. Thank God for having provided me with such a brave mother & sisters, and with such a spirit emanating [sic] from you, how could we do else but perform our duty nobly and manfully. I have never yet despaired of our cause, and notwithstanding defeats and disasters [which] attend our armies, I deem them all as being for our good, & everything that happens is for the best. There is an all-wise & overruling Providence watching our movements & whenever he sees that we are sufficiently humbled, then and not until then, will He bless our cause & send us that much-wished-for boon-Peace. Continue to pray for our country, dear mother, & also for your boys in the "Old Dominion" for our only reliance now is in prayer & through prayer only can we expect to accomplish our objects and obtain our wishes.

What a joy it must have been to behold our dear Willie once again, after such an absence. I imagine I can see our little family going wild over his arrival. Poor fellow! What a time he must have had at Point Lookout & how he will appreciate the comfort & enjoyments of our little home when he gets there; which I trust he has done ere this. Last night it was reported that Wilmington [North Carolina] had been evacuated. I feared that W. had been unable to get through, but there's nothing in today's paper in regard to it & I hope it is untrue. I have been expecting it & wouldn't be surprised at any time to hear of its occupation by the enemy, but it would cut us off entirely from home & communication with you then, would be interrupted effectively. This though I trust would only be for a short time & is no more than that has occurred to thousands of our brave soldiers whose homes are West of ours. I feel a little blue at the idea but it has passed off & if Wilmington is or has fallen it is for the best & I've no doubt will benefit the country, for our forces there will in all probability be brought to bear on Sherman's front, and aid [Pierre G. T.] Beauregard in his endeavors to whip the scoundrel. B.'s army is composed, I believe, principally of the Western troops & they are sadly in want of discipline and a commander in whom they have confidence. We see that [General Joseph] Johnston has been reinstated & I trust he may be able to bring them out. Unless Sherman is defeated before he forms a junction with Grant, we will have to fight terribly hard this summer. Lee though is at the head of affairs & he no doubt sees the importance of the struggle & is preparing all his energies to meet it. Our generals in the field now are all we can desire & with good troops and the blessing of Heaven attending us, we will bring matters to an end before next winter.

How much I would liked to have heard Mr. Geradieu preach for I know I'd have been pleased with his sermon. I shall read the chapter from which he took his text as soon as I have finished this letter. Mr. Thomas our chaplain gave me a testament recently, and I read several chapters in it daily.[9] We have preaching on Sunday & prayer meeting at night & it is much more pleasant to pass the time in listening to the word of God, than in doing nothing. I hope I may be always able to attend & also to receive instruction from His word & become a little more familiar with the Bible than I am at present.

Ma, you have no idea how much real good your letter has done me. I think I feel a hundred times better than any other man in the regiment, Ellie perhaps excepted. I don't think Col. Logan — who has just rec'd a letter from his "pretty" — feels any more elated, and even if he did I wouldn't envy him. Your sentiments, dear mother, are just the best things I've read lately, and if everybody only had such a mother, there'd be little talk of submission in our country. Already I've read it 3 or 4 times & will peruse it as many times again. Extracts from it are being circulated around the reg't extensively & we just bragg [sic] on "our mother" the "biggest kind."

---

9   Thomas and Geradieu do not appear on the rolls.

I am extremely glad to hear that Father is with you though sorry that he had to rush off & leave everything in the manner he did. However it may be for the best, for I'm inclined to think that the citizens of Charleston who exhibit any sympathy at all for the rebellion will be imprisoned or made to take the oath. This has been the case of the citizens of Virginia & the Yankee hatred toward So. Ca. is more intense than it is towards this state and their treatment will be in proportion to their dislike. If Mr. Garrett is left in charge I feel that it is [in] good hands & will be all right. Charleston I pray will soon be evacuated by the Yanks as it was by the British in the Revolution & then we will reoccupy it and "claim our possessions." What became of Uncle W. & Auntie, Cousin Laura, Mrs. Wightman, Maggie & other Charleston friends? Did they leave or come out with our forces? I am very curious to have particulars, for this reason think of borrowing and [illegible] coat and paying the old place a visit. I am confident that many of our businesses have turned traitors & taken the oath to uphold the Lincoln government but if this be the case I'd like to see them drowned or disposed of in some other equally unpleasant way. Many of them I know only awaited the approach of the Yanks to show the cloven foot and I venture to say that most [of] the farmers hailed their approach with gladness. Well, as Mrs. Higgins used to say, "let 'em go — they won't fight for us & they are too cowardly to fight against us & we get rid of finding them," so the advantage is on our side after all.

There is no news at all in our vicinity, though this morning we have heavy firing towards Petersburg and supposed it was the enemy demonstrating on the South Side [Railroad], probably endeavoring to open a way for our dearly beloved Sherman, who is no doubt attempting in conjunction with Grant to envelop & destroy the Army of Northern Virginia. It's a bold enterprise & if it succeeds 'twill be strange to me, and everybody else I reckon. The men in the army are spoiling for a fight & would give anything to "lock arms" with the hoards of Sherman. Most of them have been cut off from their homes & have become terribly mad at the way things are going on & swear vengeance against the whole united North. Their ire is fully aroused & when brought in contact with the Yanks, will fight with terrible earnestness. One fellow swore he'd fight on a half dollar, but being a pretty big chap,

I hesitated awhile before believing it. (Forgot to ask whether he meant a "shin-dash plaster" or a silver — half, but think 'twas the latter.)

For myself I want, a little more elbow room & guess I'd think seriously of getting it. The man that made the above remark forgot to allow for "stretching" & hence I think room for doubt.

Col. [Thomas M.] Logan told Ellie this morning that he was now a general & would leave us sometime next week, much to the regret of the regiment. He is to command Butler's old brigade of cavalry, and will make a splendid leader. His command is with Beauregard's army in front of Sherman's & being a good field for operations, will manufacture a name, that will become quite notorious, I believe.

Toni Hughes has come out from Point Lookout & is now in camp, tell Willie he looks as though his imprisonment had been a boon for his health, for 'tis hard to imagine a healthier looking fellow anywhere than he is & his appearance is as different from Willie's as day is from night. Though this may be accounted for by the fact that Willie was sick for sometime & H. was not. With the dear ones at home though W. will soon gain flesh & become as fit & hearty as before leaving home. Harin was uncertain about getting a furlough & seemed quite disappointed about it though he hadn't given up trying. It is reported here that the Yanks have quit exchanging prisoners, declaring it to be their intention to capture them all from us, and contrived to hold ours at the North. If so we ought to kill all their prisoners, & then there would be none for them to take.

Having exhausted my little stock of information I will now close. Much love to Father, sister Annie & Carrie, Willie, Harrie. Kiss Robbie for me. Tell them all to write me. Remember me to Mrs. McKay, [two names illegible], Mr. [M.] Roy, & all kind friends.[10] *Tell them to keep up good hearts, & be cheerful, for I haven't commenced to fight yet. I very much fear that I'll be unable to get this letter through, but venture to make the attempt. God bless & protect you always, Dear Mother.*

Your affectionate Son
Sammie

---

10   M. Roy (age 39) was a Scottish born merchant clerk in Charleston.
Entry for M. Roy, Charleston County, SC, Census of the population (NA Microfilm, roll 1216, 314), Records of the Census, 1860, South Carolina.

Hd. Qrs. Hampton Legion
[Monday] March 20, 1865

My darling Mother,

As another opportunity presents to send you a few lines I do so & hope the letters I sent by men who have gone to Sumpter have reached you. Oh, how long seems the time since I have heard from you — just one month today since your last & Annie's was dated.

Is Willie home? And where is Father? You told us to keep brave hearts & we have done so. Be assured we shall trust in a Higher Power, believing that all will yet come out well. The reports that have so far reached us all agree that Darlington Town [South Carolina] was not much injured by the enemy so I hope as we suffered considerably by the fall of Charleston that no injury was sustained by you at Timmonsville. A good many of our men have come in within the past few days & tell us the people who have suffered are very patriotic but those who were not molested are still badly whipped.

The recent successes we have had tho' small, had a very beneficial effect upon our army. A good many desertions have taken place from the army & principally from Ga. but they have in a measure stopt recently and a better spirit pervades all classes.

Sammie, I suppose, has given you an idea of our false alarms recently and of our Sunday morning scrape in which we fully expected to rout a force of Yanks, but no such good luck awaited us. I say good luck because we expected to surprise them. They took "time by the fetlock" & left before day. The rumor now is that an additional Corps has come [to] our side [of] the river apprehending an attack in [the] rear from us. They can come now if they like, but now we are prepared for them, the wretches can't hasten on at all. We have Pickett's Div. of Infantry & Fitz Lee's Cavalry all around us at least 10,000 men occupying a line of works that can most hold itself.

Last week [Charles P.] Porcher [Company K] had invited a lady to ride with him & not liking to go alone I concluded to accompany him, as there was a sister, grown, at the same house.[11]

11   Porcher enlisted in 1861. He was an officer cadet in Company K.
(Simpson, 1977, 406)

Miss Eunice Slater (my companion) started from home on Sammie's white, which being a trotter, the young lady soon was tired of so I changed saddles & she rode my black & was delighted with him.[12] *That evening we spent with the girls. They are very nice people residing near our camp. Miss Eunice is rather pretty with just such a pair of eyes as my little widow's. But Miss Slater isn't as pretty as Mrs. B. I heard her say she was making a tobacco bag & I shall carry it out of here certain.*

Dr. [N.P.] Green our [Assistant] Surgeon told her recently that her eyes had made a deep impression in Lt. Welch, which little remark [she] took surprisingly well. And Miss Eunice treats me with some consideration. But I have some common sense left & if all the girls told me I was good looking I should not believe one — they are terrible at fooling young inexperienced boys like Sammie.

Mother, I have nothing to write about. Since Sam has come he gives all the news & its impossible to gather anything besides the contents of his & a repetition is bothering and unpleasant to anyone. Miss Courtney Davis, the young lady Auld & I used to visit rode to camp this evening accompanied by David.[13] *She rides & looks very well; gave me an invitation to come around & spend the evening soon. I shall go (D.V.) this week and see her sure — she sings delightfully.*[14] *Some ladies living near camp have given me an invitation to attend a "sociable" tomorrow evening, to which I shall go, if nothing happens, as it isn't often I see much society & shall probably see some very pleasant "Old Dominion" girls.*

I would give $100 to receive a letter from you telling all were well. Have you heard anything from Charleston of your friends there? Of Aunt Emily, Cousin Laura, Mrs. Wightman, Mrs. Finney, and others?[15] *We have heard all the news from S.C. excepting of your section of country. How has Willie spent his time in Timmonsville? Do write a peck of letters by Willie and let me know everything of interest, and be sure to tell me of the little Widow.*

---

12   Miss Slater does not appear in the 1860 census.

13   This person remains unidentified.

14   D.V. means "God Willing" from the Latin "Deo Volente."

15   Again, the names are too generic to identify.

A week ago I accompanied Miss Lizzie Walker to a lecture in town and spent a very pleasant evening.[16] She seems to think of and act toward me as a sister & is a decidedly nice girl.

[J. G.] Parry & [G. H.] Spencer [both Company H] having nothing against them sufficient to convict them were released & on being sent back to camp made their guard drunk & escaped to the Yankees.[17] [Captain John D.] Palmer is still absent he will return about April. [D. S.] Dannelly ([acting] Lt.) has returned and forwarded his excuse for over staying to Gen. [Robert E.] Lee.[18] Tomorrow Pres. [Jefferson] Davis is to review Pickett's Division & I expect to go out with a lady if nothing happens.

It is impossible for me to think of anything to write about. Sammie & I are both well and enjoying ourselves as well as could be, growing fat, getting dreadfully lazy and indifferent and only get scared when they propose to take us out of the earthworks to fight unless we are to meet the Yankees in the open field.

Give much love to Father, Annie, Carrie, Willie, Harry and Robbie. God bless you & believe me ever.

Your affectionate Son,
Ellie

---

16 Miss Walker does not appear in the 1860 census.

17 (Simpson, 1977, 452)

18 Dannelly was one of the scouts with Welch.
Simpson, 1977, 450)

POSTSCRIPT

On April 12, 1865 Lieutenant Elliott Welch surrendered with the rest of the Hampton Legion at Appomattox Court House, Virginia. The Legion mustered 238 officers and men.

He and his younger brother Sammie returned to Charleston and rejoined their family there. At this point the Welch family records become rather sketchy. In 1867 Elliott engaged in the wholesale marketing of produce and fruit and made a good living at it. (He became the president of C. Bart & Co., from which he retired in 1916.) Elliott married Laura Spear in 1871 who bore him at least two children. On September 4, 1886, during the 1886 earthquake, his wife gave birth to twins in a tent along the Battery in Charleston.[19] (His one son, Emmons S. Welch, was living in 1938.)

Elliott Welch served as the ruling elder of the First (Scots) Presbyterian Church for 65 years. He became an active Mason after the war and served on the boards of the Charleston Bible Society, the old city hospital, the Charleston Orphan House, the William Enston Home, the Star Gospel Mission, and the Confederate Soldiers' Home (Columbia). He also served 12 years as the president of the South Carolina Agricultural Society.[20]

At age 93 (1936) Stephen Elliott Welch posed for a picture with cadet Allan Langdon Leonard, Jr. in a ceremony on Confederate Memorial day. Welch was the last surviving Confederate veteran of Charleston. He died on December 19, 1938, aged 95.[21]

---

19   Mrs. Anton Wright, "The Earthquake in Charleston, 1886," *South Carolina Historical and Genealogical Magazine*, Vol. 49, 69.

20   "S.C. Birthday," *Charleston News and Courier*, January 12, 1949, 12.

21   Undated article, probably 1949. Charleston *Post Courier*.
"S.C. Birthday," *Charleston News and Courier*, January 12, 1949, 12.

Willie started in the grocery trade a year earlier and stayed in that trade into the 1890's. He became a director of the Enterprise Bank and was a partner in the company of Welch & Eason. Samuel relocated to San Francisco before the 1900's and became a successful businessman.[22]

Henry F. Welch lived until December 3, 1949, aged 98. Harry, as his brothers affectionately referred to him, left behind a most interesting record. In his later years he insisted that he smuggled supplies through the lines to his brothers in southern South Carolina. (More than likely, he was referring to Willie's service toward the end of the war.)

Like Elliott, he joined the First Presbyterian Church and the Free Masons as well. Unlike his brother, he preferred to marry northerners. In 1880, he married Sarah Spencer (Hartford, Connecticut). She died shortly thereafter. He then wed Jessie Williams (Glastonbury, Connecticut), who died in 1902. In 1911, when he was 60 years old, he married Margaret E. Hughes of Marion, Ohio, who survived him, as did his two sons, Norman Spencer and Henry Hughes Welch.[23]

---

22   (Evans, 1987, 903-905)

23   "Henry F. Welch Dies at 98, Funeral Rites to Be Today," *Charleston News and Courier*, December 4, 1949, 2A.

BIBLIOGRAPHY

Adjutant General's Office, *Official Army Register of the Volunteer Force of the United States Army*, Part VIII (Gaithersburg, Md.: Ron Van Sickle Military Books, 1987)

Charleston Post Courier, undated article (probably 1949)

Evans, Clement A., (ed.), *Confederate Military History Extended Edition*, "South Carolina," VI. (Wilmington, Del.: Broadfoot Publishing, 1987)

"Henry F. Welch Dies at 98, Funeral Rites to be Today," *Charleston News and Courier*, December 4, 1949, 2A.

Johnson, Robert U. and Clarence Buel, (eds.), *Battles and Leaders of the Civil War*, IV, (Secaucus: Castle Books)

Krick, Robert K., *Lee's Colonels* (Dayton, Oh.: Morningside Press, 1979)

Longstreet, James, *From Manassas to Appomattox* (N.Y.: DaCapo, 1992)

Polley, J. B., *Hood's Texas Brigade* (Dayton, Oh.: Morningside Books, 1976)

Priest, John M., *Antietam: The Soldiers' Battle* (Shippensburg, Pa.: White Mane Publishing, 1989)

Priest, John M., *Before Antietam: The Battle for South Mountain* (Shippensburg, Pa.: White Mane Publishing, 1992)

Rosters of the 7th South Carolina Cavalry, 8th Battalion South Carolina Reserves, and the Hampton Legion, Microfilm Room, National Archives, Washington, DC

Scott, Robert, (comp.), *The Official Records of the War of the Rebellion*, Vol. XLII, part 1 (Washington, DC: U.S. Government Printing Office)

Simpson, Harold B., *Hood's Texas Brigade: A Compendium*, (Hillsboro, Texas: Hill Junior College, 1977)

Simpson, Harold P., *Hood's Texas Brigade: Lee's Grenadier Guard* (Dallas, Texas: Alcor Publishing Co., 1983)

"S.C. Birthday," *Charleston News and Courier*, January 12, 1949, 12.

Warner, Ezra, *Generals in Blue* (Baton Rouge, La.: Louisiana State University Press, 1964)

Wright, Mrs. Anton, "The Earthquake in Charleston, 1886," *South Carolina Historical and Genealogical Magazine*, Vols. 49 and 69.

INDEX